Saint Gianna and Pietro Molla Maternity Home:

A STORY OF FAITH, HOPE AND *joy*

SAINT GIANNA & PIETRO MOLLA
Maternity Home

UNIVERSITY
of MARY PRESS

Written by Rebecca Crooks

Published in the United States of America
by University of Mary Press
7500 University Drive
Bismarck, ND 58504
www.umary.edu

ISBN: 978-1-7348826-6-7

Foreward

We are excited to share this book with you. The task of putting together a history of the work of Saint Gianna and Pietro Molla Maternity Home is not a small one! Rebecca Crooks had the heart and the skills to compile a snapshot and synopsis of these past 20 years. Becca weaves together many different people's stories and experiences. Each mother and each child as well as each board member, staff member and supporter has taught me of the Lord's goodness and love so beautifully expressed on these pages. I am humbled to have witnessed what God has done in the hearts and lives of so many people who have been touched by the work of Saint Gianna and Pietro's Molla Maternity Home in the tiny village of Warsaw, North Dakota. I am grateful to the University of Mary for helping us to publish this book, and to Becca Crooks for sharing her talent, and to everyone who helped make this Home and this book a reality.

Mary Pat Jahner
Director, Saint Gianna and Pietro Molla Maternity Home

"Lord, Let the light that has been lit in my soul never be extinguished."- Saint Gianna

Acknowledgments

While the amount of time I spent working at Saint Gianna and Pietro Molla Maternity Home as a housemother is minimal compared to the work of others involved, I grew up 'alongside' the Maternity Home, as it was then known. The Home opened while I was attending Minto High School and my mother has been the office manager for as long as I can remember. Over the past twenty years, it has become part of the landscape that I call home, the place that I come from. Because of this, I have heard countless stories of God's

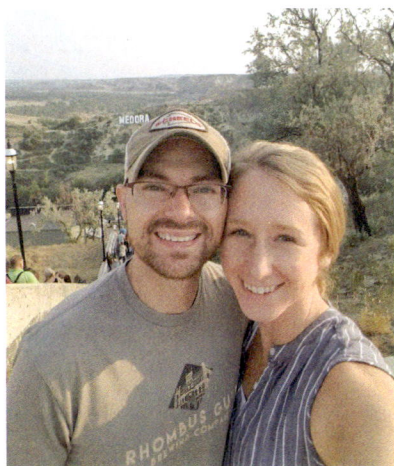

John & Rebecca Crooks.

providence and the generosity of people over the years. Writing its history and the stories of those involved has been a great honor for me.

Documenting the beginning years of the Home's work and all that follows would not have been possible without a number of people. I would like to thank Mary Pat Jahner, who accepted my proposal to write this book several years ago and answered question after question about the history, people, and timeline. I would also like to thank Father Joseph Christensen for his close reading of the draft and each comma he added. I would also like to thank Anne Dunn and Viana Schlapp for sharing their time in editing the manuscript.

I would like to thank my parents, Don and Susan Barclay, whose example of generosity is one of the greatest gifts I have received. These pages tell the story of God's great generosity with us and the impact of the generosity of others. The telling would not be possible without the gift of life I received and this includes being able to recognize the beauty and goodness of living generously in your community.

I would like to thank my husband, John, whose support is a great constant in my life. He has always encouraged me to write and reminds me regularly that I have stories to share. Learning to live a life of generosity alongside him is my greatest joy.

Lastly, I would like to thank everyone who trusted me with their story for this project. The stories in this book are personal. They tell about moments of pain and joy, times of darkness and light in a person's life. These stories are treasures and I have done my best to share them for what they are. Holding them in my heart and writing about them for others has been an invitation for me to see God's goodness in the world. I hope it is the same for all those who read them.

Rebecca Crooks

Introduction

Over twenty years ago, the seed was planted for a maternity home on the prairie of North Dakota. At the time, those involved could hardly imagine the extent of the good that would come from a seed as small as desiring to love and help one mother, one baby, and one family at a time.

The Saint Gianna and Pietro Molla Maternity Home brings the beautiful pro-life message to all who encounter this home in the small town of Warsaw, North Dakota. The staff lives with pregnant mothers and their little ones and works with former residents and their families. The heart of the staff's mission is loving the mothers and children whose lives are often shrouded in difficulty and walking with them in their joys and sufferings. This deeply spiritual mission attracts those who visit the Home—many people who make pilgrimages here experience suffering, whether it be difficult pregnancies or the pain of infertility. They come to the Home praying for miracles, finding strength and healing on their knees at the Saint Gianna shrine, located in the Visitation Chapel on the main floor. Saint Gianna and her holy husband Pietro intercede tirelessly for those who ask for prayers at the Maternity Home, strengthening these individuals in their faith.

The lives of Saint Gianna and her husband Pietro inspire the ministry of the Saint Gianna and Pietro Molla Maternity Home, which serves mothers and their children with the belief that each life is a precious gift from God. The people who encounter the Home witness the spirit of this holy couple and their great devotion to the sanctity of life. This small maternity home, geographically located in the middle of nowhere, embodies the virtues dear to Saint Gianna's heart — compassion for others, complete trust in the will of God, and serving with a generous heart. At the Home, no task or life is unimportant in the eyes of God, and each day is a stepping stone on the path of holiness.

What started as "Blessed Gianna's Maternity Home" has blossomed, first to "Saint Gianna's Maternity Home," as Gianna Molla was canonized a saint shortly after the doors to the Maternity Home opened. Now, in conjunction with celebrating twenty years of saving mothers, babies, and families, the Maternity Home has been renamed again to "Saint Gianna and Pietro Molla Maternity Home." While it is indeed a 'change' in name, this change more truly captures the work of the Home.

Saint Gianna and Pietro's daughter, Doctor Gianna Emanuela, is a dear friend of the Maternity Home and it was her text to Mary Pat Jahner, inspired by the Holy Spirit, that led to this name change. "Maybe you can consider recalling the Home: Saint Gianna and Pietro Maternity Home!" she wrote after she had prayed fervently for her saintly parents' intercession for a successful Giving Hearts Day in February 2022.

"We had never considered this before," Mary Pat said. "We love and honor and ask for the intercession of Pietro Molla so much and yet the idea to rename our home had never crossed my mind! I presented the idea to Father Joseph Christensen, and he wholeheartedly agreed as well. From there, we began to take steps to work towards this change, shocking people initially when we would say we were thinking about changing the name (because everyone knows how much we love Saint Gianna), but then seeing them rejoice with the addition of her saintly husband."

"According to God's will, I couldn't get to know my Mom personally; however, the Lord, in His infinite goodness, granted me the extraordinary grace to live with my Dad for the longest time of 48 years of my life," Gianna Emanuela said. "He became both Mom and Dad to me and my siblings. All these years I could see his example with my own eyes; this has been for me so very important, a true blessing! While living with him, I completely understood why my Saint Mom took an example from him and learned what it means to be a 'saint of everyday life.' His life and writings reveal that his soul was totally immersed in God; that his unshakable faith permeated and strengthened every single aspect of his life."

This saintly man was instrumental to his wife Gianna becoming a Saint, and his example and intercession have been a regular part of the Maternity Home's functioning since its beginning.

Pietro Molla was chosen and greatly loved by Saint Gianna, who was the first to recognize and proclaim his holy example. The story and virtues of Saint Gianna are intertwined with her beloved spouse, and incomplete without him. Saint Gianna and Pietro offer us a beautiful example of the self-giving sacrament and show us the fruits of building a family with faith as an unshakable foundation. Pietro, an exemplary father, serves as a beautiful inspiration to fathers everywhere. Our work exists because the women and children we serve often lack holy and strong fathers and husbands like Pietro.

Pietro Molla and Gianna Emanuela Molla on September 25, 2002, hold the image of then Blessed Gianna's Maternity Home that was presented to them at their home in Italy. Presented by Archbishop Aquila, Father Damian Hils, Colleen Samson, and Mary Pat Jahner.

Pietro Molla was a single parent and a strong example for the mothers we serve. And we would like to be a part of promoting devotion to Pietro Molla in hope that his Cause for Beatification and Canonization would be opened, and more people would come to know and love him along with his Saint wife, Gianna.

"How many times has my Dad repeated these words to me: 'Jesus Christ came on this earth to serve, not to be served, and we must do the same. The purpose of our life on this earth is to do good to our neighbor. At the last of our earthly days, we will be judged by the Lord on the basis of love,'" shared Gianna Emanuela. "I am happy to share my saintly parents with the world; with their growing number of spiritual children, and, even more so with all people who pray to them and ask for their intercession: I join my prayers to theirs! May their example enlighten our daily journey towards holiness and Heaven; inspire the Christian journey of young people, fiancées, spouses, parents, widowers, families, and every person; be a source of strength, courage, support, and consolation along life's trials, difficulties, and sufferings; give much hope and renew, every day of our life, our full and complete confidence in Divine Providence."

In a world that increasingly removes God and faith from the public sphere, the lives of the saints provide a courageous example in a secular world. The saints show the beauty of a life lived radically in love with Christ.

Saint Gianna lived a full life, completely dedicated to the love of God and others. Gianna attained the glory of sainthood by serving her husband, children, and patients with great faithfulness and joy in the resurrected Christ. Gianna invited the Holy Spirit to transform her daily life into moments of holiness. Her actions united with a firm disposition to do good, allowed virtue to weave meaning into the ordinary and mundane. The glory of the saints lies in their great love of God, regardless of their time or place in history. By loving God, they have become beacons of love incarnate in the Church.

Only a short time ago, not many knew of Gianna and the Molla family.

For the Molla family, life went on after the death of Gianna in 1962. Pietro had the task of continuing to provide for his family while also raising their children. It is rare that the Canonization of a saint happens while her contemporaries are still living, much rarer to find that it is her husband and children who promote her cause and attend the Canonization. It was quickly made known to the Church and the world that Gianna's life was an example for all who live in our world today.

May 16, 2004 Saint Gianna's canonization day. Pope Saint John Paul II greets Pietro and Gianna Emanuela Molla.

Mere decades after her death, Saint Gianna is a patron for mothers, family life, doctors, the pro-life movement, and more. People all over the world have been encouraged and inspired by her life of faith, hope, and joy.

Saint Gianna's final acts were those of honoring and respecting her baby's life, sacrificing her own life for the sake of that baby, and trusting in God's providence. Each of these actions was rooted in a lifetime of virtue. They were rooted in a great hope in God, a firm disposition to do good, and a desire to do right by God and others.

A Whole Life of Love

When people of faith look at Saint Gianna's life, they are encouraged by this woman's path to sainthood, in which God's grace colors the mundaneness of everyday life. In Saint Gianna — Her Life of Joy and Heroic Sacrifice, Giuliana Pelucchi invites us into the story of Saint Gianna, whose beautiful life shows the holiness that can grow in the ordinary with the help of God's grace.

In 1922 in Magenta, Italy, the Beretta family unknowingly welcomed a future saint into their home: a beautiful baby girl named Gianna. Gianna was the tenth of thirteen children born to Alberto and Maria Beretta, devout Catholics who loved their faith and spent their lives passing this faith on to their children. God's love filled the Beretta home from the time Gianna was a baby, and faith and familial love greatly blessed the Beretta children.

Gianna's older brother, Ferdinando, recalls their parents' approach to educating their children in the faith: "My father and my mother were very attentive to our formation, but they left us free to learn on our own the value of what they taught us."[1] Alberto and Maria embraced their parental role as the primary educators of their children in the Catholic faith, teaching their children by exemplifying good and holy lives. The faith began at home for Gianna and her siblings, who were taught to individually embrace God in their own lives. The Beretta children sought to share the love of God and respect all of God's children made in His image and likeness. Alberto and Maria's children grew into young adults who cultivated their Catholic faith, despite the political uncertainty and Fascist rule that prevailed around them for the first twenty years of Gianna's life. For the Beretta family, the Catholic faith invited their children to counter the grim political climate against the joy of the Gospel.

Tragedy struck the Beretta family with the death of Gianna's oldest sister, Amelia, in 1937. Amelia had been ill for some time, and Gianna and her family experienced great sorrow at her passing. As she mourned the loss of her sister, Gianna's sufferings were accompanied by a great deepening of faith through the grace of God. Only fifteen years old, Gianna began to direct her thoughts toward eternal life in Heaven through daily meditation and prayer.

The loss of Amelia was the beginning of a season of changes for the Beretta family. Shortly after her death, they moved to Genova due to Alberto's continual struggle with pernicious anemia. Beyond the walls of Gianna's home, tensions rose as war loomed on the horizon. It wouldn't be long before the Beretta family would experience living in a world at war.

In 1942, a few years after Amelia's death, Gianna's mother and father passed away. Maria's unexpected death occurred first, caused by a cerebral hemorrhage. Alberto passed away a few months after his wife, ending his longtime struggle with anemia.[2] The loss of their parents bound the Beretta children closer than ever. Together they agreed to move to Magenta, taking up residence in their paternal grandparents' house.

These challenging years required a deepening of trust in God's providence as the Berettas weathered the changing world around them, without their parents and sister. Instead of becoming disheartened and destitute, the faith of the Beretta children continued to grow. The seeds of faith that Alberto and Maria planted in their children's hearts were deeply rooted and persisted despite their suffering. Their experiences of loss and uncertainty invited them to share in the sufferings of Jesus on the Cross and experience the companionship of Christ in their mourning.

The losses Gianna encountered did not paralyze her in sullenness and doubt. A true saint, Gianna's suffering became integral to her spiritual growth as a young woman. Gianna continued to spend time in daily prayer and focus her life on the one thing that mattered — union with Christ on earth in hopes of the eternal reward of Heaven.

Gianna enrolled in medical school shortly after the death of her parents. In this way, she followed the path of her brothers Ferdinando and Enrico (who took the name Alberto when he became a Capuchin priest and is now Venerable). Gianna's pursuit of medicine taught her how to physically care for her patients and offer the healing love of Christ to each person she met. As a doctor, Gianna treated each person with dignity and respect based on her belief that each person she met bore the image of the Creator. Gianna believed in the great love God has for His creation, and found great joy in caring for His children. The field of medicine offered Gianna consolation and joy in loving others, especially those most in need.

Gianna faced the same questions of career and vocation encountered by all young adults. Gianna's twenties and early thirties were a time of great growth, as Gianna discerned God's calling for her life and the ways she could use her talents for His glory. She was confident in pursuing the qualifications to become a doctor, and considered providing care for the poorest of the poor as a missionary alongside her brother Father Alberto in Brazil. While discerning where to practice medicine, Gianna built a healthcare practice in Mesero, Italy. In Saint Gianna's biography, Pelucchi writes that Gianna "learned a valuable lesson in her youth: to share the fruits of this love, these gifts that she had received, with those who were less fortunate." [3] Gianna found great purpose in the medical field, especially in helping women and children who needed support and encouragement along with medical care. While Gianna remained uncertain of her vocation and next career steps, her belief in God's goodness persisted, allowing her to joyfully serve others.

Pietro and Saint Gianna in Taormina, Italy in October of 1955.

Faith became accessible in Gianna's daily life by trusting everything to Divine Providence. Her remarkable openness to each person she met accompanied her joyful spirit as she engaged with her patients. Little did she know the ways her life would soon change as a wife and mother.

Gianna met Pietro Molla and spent time with his family over the course of several months. Pietro, a faith-filled man, was a perfect match for Gianna. The two fell in love and were ready to embark on a life together in pursuit of Heaven. Saint Gianna married Pietro at the age of thirty-two. The time Gianna spent treating her patients as a single woman paved the way for her God-given vocation as a wife and mother. In this new vocation, Gianna felt God calling her to share generously with Pietro and the children they would be blessed with.

In Gianna's own words addressed to Pietro, she speaks of the way trust and doubt weave

> "There will be sorrows, too, of course, but if we always *love each other* as we do now, then, with God's help, we'll know how to bear them together."

together to form a life of faith: "There will be sorrows, too, of course, but if we always love each other as we do now, then, with God's help, we'll know how to bear them together." [4] From this short account of Gianna's life, it becomes clear that she spent her lifetime learning how to live with great love. It wasn't only Gianna's heroic sacrifice at the end of her final pregnancy that made her a saint, but the holiness seeping out of her daily life.

Many view Saint Gianna's holiness in terms of her final act of love - the choice to give her unborn child life, in exchange for her own. Gianna's final pregnancy revealed the magnitude of her heart, but these great depths of love grew alongside her unborn daughter Gianna Emanuela. Gianna's final act perfectly embodies the

St. Gianna & Pietro in Sestriere, Italy, April 1955.

Christian call to lay down one's life out of love, and was built on a lifetime of habitual virtue and sacrifice. Each daily act of faith, hope, and charity deepened the virtues planted in Gianna by the Beretta family. These virtues were cultivated throughout Gianna's adolescence and medical studies, and blossomed in her adulthood, marriage, and motherhood.

Saint Gianna's life reveals the ways love can grow in the repetition of small acts of love and the habitual choice of trusting in God's providence. This love is grounded in the dignity of each human life and hope in the joys of eternal salvation. The sacrifices required of her at each stage of life fell upon a heart that was open to receive. Gianna's life, prior to her final sacrifice, was a very common life marked by otherworldly hope and great joy.

The Catholic Church lifts Saint Gianna as a holy woman, with emphasis on her great virtue accompanying the sacrifices she made. Saint Gianna serves as an approachable saint who holds a kind of familiarity to modern viewers. Gianna's legacy remains that of a kind woman with a love for serving others; a doctor marked by generosity and diligence; a wife and mother who embraced sacrifice and deeply understood the beauty of the gift of life. The presence of Gianna's faith brings her to life as a real member of the Communion of Saints who will not tire in interceding for God's children who ask her help.

Few will have to make the ultimate sacrifice of giving their life for another in love, but each person can learn from Saint Gianna's good and beautiful example. Her courage and faith as a young girl who lost her sister and parents inspires Catholics to turn to the Lord for a deepening of faith in times of strife. Her receptiveness to the will of God invites men and women at all stages in life to deepen their trust in the Lord. Gianna's desire to live as a servant of Christ shows the faithful how to pour themselves out in service of others, the way she did as a doctor, wife, and mother until her last moments.

Pietro and Saint Gianna with Pierluigi in Courmayeur, Italy 1957.

A Story of Faith

Gianna's sainthood lies in her great faith, the same faith that inspired countless saints before her. Unwavering trust in God characterized her life and final pregnancy. Gianna's faithful cooperation with God challenges a secular world that wrongly understands faith as something requiring complete knowledge of God. The faith requires not complete certainty, but a humble acceptance of human limitations made beautiful by the infinite grace of a Heavenly Creator. The Catholic Church teaches that God has created humans to love and serve Him; the theological virtues strengthens man in his relationship with God, as explained by the Catechism of the Catholic Church:

"The human virtues are rooted in the theological virtues, which adapt man's faculties for participation in the divine nature: for the theological virtues relate directly to God. They dispose Christians to live in a relationship with the Holy Trinity. They have the One and Triune God for their origin, motive, and object.

The theological virtues are the foundation of Christian moral activity; they animate it and give it its special character. They inform and give life to all the moral virtues. They are infused by God into the souls of the faithful to make them capable of acting as his children and of meriting eternal life. They are the pledge of the presence and action of the Holy Spirit in the faculties of the human being. There are three theological virtues: faith, hope, and charity." (Catechism of the Catholic Church, 1812-13)

From this understanding, partaking in the theological virtues of faith, hope, and charity is integral to living in relationship with God. Through these God-given gifts, Catholics can participate in God's life on earth and come to know Him in a deeper way. The first of these virtues is faith,

"Faith is the theological virtue by which we believe in God and believe all that He has said and revealed to us, and that Holy Church proposes for our belief because He is truth itself. By faith 'man freely commits his entire self to God.' For this reason, the believer seeks to know and do God's Will." (Catechism of the Catholic Church, 1814-15).

Faith is not weak or foolishness as the secular world defines it. Instead of existing separate from reason, faith is truth itself and the fullness of understanding. It is saints like Gianna who show the greatness of faith given by God to His beloved children, so that they may love and serve Him with great fervor. Furthermore, a life without faith will be fruitless, as the person tries to sever every tie with the One whom he is made by and for. A saint's great example of love points to the Divine, while a faithless life defies the ultimate purpose of mankind – unification with God, who is Love Incarnate.

The life of Saint Gianna reveals a great paradox of faith. Faith, the key to a personal relationship with God, invites man to surrender everything to the Father with full confidence in His goodness. In the eyes of the world this appears foolish, but in reality faith allows the believer to open their eyes and live for Heaven.

The theological virtue of hope sustains faith. The virtue of hope ties fulfillment to eternal salvation rather than this world,

> "The virtue of hope responds to the aspiration to happiness which God has placed in the heart of every man; it takes up the hopes that inspire men's activities and purifies them so as to order them to the Kingdom of Heaven; it keeps man from discouragement; it sustains him during times of abandonment; it opens up his heart in expectation of eternal beatitude. Buoyed up by hope, he is preserved from selfishness and led to the happiness that flows from charity." (Catechism of the Catholic Church, 1818)

Hope is not naive ignorance of the difficulties of this world. Rather, this virtue points to the deep fulfillment that will only be fully experienced in eternity. Hope is the anchor allowing people of faith to weather the waves of uncertainty while living amongst passing things. It helps the faithful distinguish between worldly and eternal things.

Desiring the eternal over the temporary allows Christians to live out their call to love God and their neighbors in the imitation of Christ. Christians, marked with an otherworldly joy, have the fullness of hope because of eternal salvation, "By hope we desire, and with steadfast trust await from God, eternal life and the graces to merit it" (Catechism of the Catholic Church, 1843).

Hope purified Saint Gianna and ordered her dreams and love for her family towards the Kingdom of Heaven. The virtue of hope anchored her to the truth of God's love for herself and her unborn baby. Hope mediated Gianna's sacrifice of earthly goods in exchange for the eternal goodness of God Himself.

Saint Gianna's cancer diagnosis during her pregnancy gave her months to prepare for the possibility of sacrificing her life out of love for her unborn child. Even with the heartbreaking prospect of leaving her earthly family, Gianna did not lose hope in God's goodness.

The life of Saint Gianna, first and foremost, is one of love. This virtue "upholds and purifies our human ability to love and raises it to the supernatural perfection of divine love" (Catechism of the Catholic Church, 1827). God, in His goodness, can purify each act of love. Sanctity lies in inviting God to purify even the smallest acts of love.

A life rooted in the theological virtues of faith, hope, and charity reveals the tremendous gifts of the Holy Spirit: "The fruits of the Spirit are perfections that the Holy Spirit forms in us as the first fruits of eternal glory," (Catechism of the Catholic Church, 1832). Where love is purified, the Holy Spirit presides, and God's children experience a small taste of Heaven.

The lives of the saints are marked by the gift of joy. When such faith and hope is rooted together in the Christian heart, an other-worldly joy is present. Despite worldly troubles, the faith and hope of the saints anchored their lives to the eternal, allowing them to experience a joy on earth that will only be matched in Heaven. Saint Gianna undoubtedly faced deep sadness at the prospect of dying before her children were raised, however, she remained joyful to the end because of her relationship with God, who is the fullness of truth and love.

A Seed Is Planted

From Christmas Eve 1999 through the Epiphany on January 6, 2001, Catholic Christians across the world celebrated the great Jubilee Year. The turning of the century was a momentous occasion in many ways. It was no different for the life of the Church.

Leading up to the Jubilee Year, Saint John Paul II invited Christians all over the globe to "respect the measurements of time" as the Church sought to help everyone "to realize how each of these measurements of time is imbued with the presence of God and with his saving activity." [5]

The Jubilee Year was a celebration of two thousand years of God's presence and saving activity in the Church. It served as an opportunity to remember Christ's birth into a particular time and place in history and reflect on what the Incarnation means for us as Christians.

In his address, Tertio Millenio Adveniente on the coming of the third millennium, Saint John Paul II explains to us the reason for a jubilee celebration:

"The term "Jubilee" speaks of joy; not just an inner joy but a jubilation which is manifested outwardly, for the coming of God is also an outward, visible, audible, and tangible event, as Saint John makes clear (cf. 1 Jn 1:1). It is thus appropriate that every sign of joy at this coming should have its own outward expression. This will demonstrate that the Church rejoices in salvation. She invites everyone to rejoice, and she tries to create conditions to ensure that the power of salvation may be shared by all.

It is aimed at an increased sensitivity to all that the Spirit is saying to the Church and to the Churches (cf. Rev 2:7 ff.), as well as to individuals through charisms meant to serve the whole community. The purpose is to emphasize what the Spirit is suggesting to the different communities, from the smallest ones, such as the family, to the largest ones, such as nations and international organizations, taking into account cultures, societies, and sound traditions." [6]

The Great Jubilee celebration was a yearlong invitation for Christians to discern how to further God's saving mission in the world. This celebration provided a special occasion for Christians to unify and sanctify their time. As Saint John Paul II said, this work of listening to the Holy Spirit was necessary for everyone, from families to whole nations. These words remind Christians of their special responsibility to listen to the Holy Spirit. In doing this, God guides His children to share their gifts and talents with their families and communities.

As the Jubilee Year was coming to its close, the Holy Spirit was working in rural North Dakota; while the dedication of Blessed Gianna's Maternity Home was in August 2003, the seed for its beginning was planted in the year 2000. The Feast of Our Lady of Guadalupe, December 12, 2000, is considered the spiritual birthday of the Maternity Home. On this feast day of the Patroness of the Unborn, an idea was shared that set the Home in motion.

The beginning of the Maternity Home's story is marked by a great openness to the Holy Spirit and willingness to use individual charisms to serve the community.

The Maternity Home fulfilled Saint John Paul II's words concerning the Jubilee Year. It became a sign of joy for the community of Warsaw, North Dakota, and beyond, for all those who would become part of the Saint Gianna and Pietro Molla Home family.

Mary Pat with Aubrey, 3 years old, at the time of Aubrey's adoption.

Nothing Practical

Mary Pat Jahner, originally from Dickinson, North Dakota, received her bachelor's degree in Elementary Education from Dickinson State University and her Master's in Theological Studies from the Institute of Religious and Pastoral Studies Program. She was an educator for 12 years, working in South Dakota; the Fargo Catholic Schools Network; Belcourt, North Dakota; and East Grand Forks, Minnesota.

Each summer Mary Pat would spend time doing mission work. During the summer of 1998, she had hoped to work in an orphanage in a third-world country, however, God had other plans. The cost of an international plane ticket barred her from serving abroad but led her to an experience that would lay the foundation for Saint Gianna's Maternity Home.

Mary Pat spent the summer in Los Angeles, California with the Missionaries of Charity. While it was not an orphanage, the Sisters ran a maternity shelter taking in women and children off the streets and showing them the love of Christ. This experience gave Mary Pat a close-up look at the ways to love and serve vulnerable women. In her words, "Even if the women who were served went back to where they came from, they knew and experienced real love and real care while they were with the Sisters."

Having witnessed the Missionaries of Charity's immense love for women and children, Mary Pat recognized the need to support mothers and children in all communities, including her home state. While North Dakota varied from California in population and landscape, there were still women who found themselves in unexpected pregnancies without the support any mother would need. Mary Pat's work as a teacher exposed her to the reality of young women and former students who didn't have support in bringing life into the world and raising their children surrounded by difficulty.

Mary Pat believed that a maternity home was needed in North Dakota. In her mind, this wasn't just a place for women to have their babies and leave, but rather a home for women and children to experience Christ's healing love. In coming to the Home, the women would be welcomed into a family. The Home Mary Pat envisioned would not simply offer clothing, shelter, and food. It had to offer more — the love of Christ to all who needed it.

After her summer volunteer work with the Missionaries of Charity, Mary Pat took a one-year leave of absence from her Fargo teaching position and taught second graders in Belcourt on the Turtle Mountain Indian Reservation.

As Mary Pat prepared her second graders for their first reconciliation, she planned a retreat day for them with a priest she knew from working in the Fargo Catholic Schools Network. This priest, Father Damian Hils, had been in Fargo for two years before being called to serve as the pastor at Saint Stanislaus Parish in Warsaw, North Dakota.

Originally from northern Kentucky, Father Hils was raised in a Catholic home. After high school, he received his bachelor's degree in history from Thomas More College in Kentucky and a Master's degree in medieval history from the University of Notre Dame. Father Hils completed one year of architecture work before responding to his vocation to the priesthood.

Having learned of the Red River Valley through a research project on Bishop William Mulloy of Covington, KY, Father Hils spent time traveling through North Dakota, where Bishop Mulloy had served in Grafton and Ardoch. While traveling through this area, he frequently stopped at Saint Stanislaus, known as the Cathedral of the Prairie, to pray and appreciate the beautiful architecture.

It was a cold winter day in December of 2000 when Father Hils made his way to Belcourt to offer the day of recollection for Mary Pat's second graders. At the end of the reconciliation retreat, around 3:00 p.m. the Hour of Mercy, Father Hils asked Mary Pat a small question that would have large repercussions.

"What do you plan to do at the end of the school year?" he asked. "Will you go back to Shanley or stay here in Belcourt?"

Mary Pat was surprised by the question because it was the middle of the school year. Contracts did not need to be signed until the spring which was still months away. When Mary Pat didn't respond right away, Father Hils asked, "Or something else?"

To which she responded, "Nothing practical."

Father Hils listened intently to Mary Pat's "impractical" plans as she shared the stirrings of her heart and belief that there was a great need for a maternity home in North Dakota. Thankfully, Father Hils was a man who was not afraid to set aside practicality in pursuit of God's will. In response, Father Hils asked another question.

"How about Warsaw?"

Father Hils had lived in Warsaw for the past three years. Just across

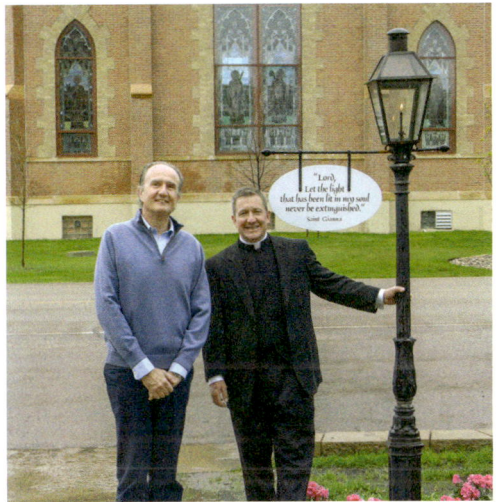

Pierluigi Molla with Father Damian Hils outside of our Home.

the street from Saint Stanislaus sat a large, dilapidated building. Originally a convent and boarding school, the building that is now Saint Gianna and Pietro Molla Maternity Home has a long history of holy efforts, but in the year 2000, the building sat empty. The Sisters of the Resurrection had originally built a convent that opened in 1921 and stayed in the community until 1971, when Saint Anthony's School and Convent closed.

Since then, a few efforts had been made to use the building, but nothing had lasted. After Father Hils' arrival in Warsaw, the Bishop had asked for a handful of ideas for the building. One of his ideas was a maternity home. In this one conversation, both Father Hils' idea for a maternity home in Warsaw and Mary Pat's vision for a home for mothers in North Dakota became a possibility.

In the recollections of Mary Pat and Father Hils, it becomes clear that Divine Providence was guiding the way for them to begin a maternity home in Warsaw. Father Hils provided counsel on the location and building that could house the future mothers and children who would become the life of the Home. He also knew the next person Mary Pat should speak to if she was serious about the idea: Colleen Samson.

Colleen Samson, a resident of Park River, North Dakota, met Father Hils through her mother, Irene Schanilec. Irene was a volunteer sacristan at Saint Luke's and enjoyed having the parish priest as her guest. Father Hils met Irene's family and children, including Colleen, through these visits, and she remembers him fondly: "Father Hils was instrumental in organizing conferences at [Saint Luke's and Saint Stanislaus], and we were delighted to attend them with our children and as adults," said Colleen Samson. "He was very committed to the pro-life cause."

Colleen has a great love for the pro-life cause and spent her adult life working to enshrine the dignity of the human person. Feeling God's invitation into the pro-life arena, Colleen's pro-life activity has spanned over thirty years. Alongside raising seven children, she was involved with her local Right to Life Chapter before becoming Director at the Pregnancy Help Center in Park River, ND.

"The Pregnancy Help Center had discussed the possibility of a maternity home in our area, and we committed this possibility to prayer and to God," said Colleen. "What a beautiful surprise to meet someone [Mary Pat] sent to us by God for this very purpose. It was a lovely meeting, and I could see the commitment she was willing to undergo to make this dream a reality."

"I spoke with Colleen Samson on January 6, 2001," said Mary Pat. "It was the last day of the Jubilee year which is remarkable to think about in the whole realm of Church history." When looking at the beginnings of the Maternity Home, a deep sense of Divine Providence weaves its way throughout the stories. As the plans for the Home unfolded and took shape, it would be the combination of many people and their gifts that would breathe life into this life-giving apostolate.

After Colleen and Mary Pat discussed the idea of the Home, they soon realized that the success of the Home would first require the Bishop's support and approval.

"Father Hils recommended we visit Bishop Sullivan regarding the venture in order to seek his wisdom and consent," shared Colleen.

The Maternity Home would not be formally associated with the Diocese of Fargo but serve as a Catholic apostolate. The Bishop's approval would invite both the lay faithful and the priests of the Diocese to support and recommend the Home to women in their communities.

Recognizing the need to show the Bishop that there would be support behind the idea, Mary Pat recalls attending this meeting with Karen Hofer, who, along with her husband Mike Hofer, were active as business entrepreneurs, faithful Catholics, and generous supporters in the Fargo Diocese and the Fargo Catholic Schools Network.

One can see from the inception of the Home that God uses not only our desires and talents but also the personal connections we make through life to bring about His will. Mary Pat's time as a teacher and her involvement with the Catholic Church as a young woman created a number of connections that would allow the Home to come to life.

One of those connections that provided much-needed support in the Catholic community of the Fargo Diocese was Mary Pat's relationship with Mike and Karen Hofer. The Hofer's, Fargo residents, were raising their three children while Mary Pat taught in the Fargo Catholic Schools. Mary Pat taught two of their sons in junior high and high school and had also babysat their kids.

"Mike and I were not surprised when she told us about her interest in starting a home for women in crisis pregnancies because Mary Pat was always helping everyone," said Karen Hofer. "We didn't even think twice about helping. We really felt that if she felt that strongly about it and after visiting with her and Father Damian, we knew it was the right thing to do."

Mike and Karen's familiarity with starting businesses, generosity in the Catholic community, and relationship with the Diocese of Fargo provided the support Mary Pat and Father Hils needed to transition the Mternity Home from a hope to a reality in the Diocese.

"We always admired Mary Pat and thought the world of her," Karen shared. "When she mentioned to us the idea of starting a Blessed Gianna Maternity Home, we were totally unaware of who Blessed Gianna was and we were not familiar with the Molla family history. We backed her desire to do this wholeheartedly because we knew she was such a good person and she felt very strongly about the endeavor. We decided to support the project because it tugged at our hearts to do something to get it started."

Each conversation or interaction with another, no matter how short, is an opportunity to bring Christ's presence to others. As our culture grows increasingly focused on efficiency and speed, it can be easy to forget the power of presence. Presence is at the center of the Catholic faith, particularly the presence of Jesus Christ in the most holy Eucharist. Through the institution of the Eucharist, Christ gave the world His continued presence in the Mass, adoration, and in tabernacles throughout the world. Christ's presence is both a promise and a calling. Christ instituted the Eucharist as a way to remain with and in Him. Christ's mercy and steadfast love are demonstrated through the Eucharist. In return, those Christ calls are tasked with being His hands, feet, and eyes in the world.

Allowing Christ to permeate every aspect of life makes it easier to feel God's "tug of the heart" and respond to His call — just as Mike and Karen Hofer did. By supporting Mary Pat and Father Hils with their presence, talents, and treasure, Mike and Karen invited others to consider it as a viable possibility and a cause worthy of consideration for the Fargo Diocese in North Dakota.

After seeing support and encouragement from various people, Bishop Sullivan gave his blessing for the endeavor. Mike Hofer agreed to serve as the first President of the Board of Directors for the Maternity Home.

"We met with Bishop Sullivan – Colleen Samson, Karen Hofer, and myself," said Mary Pat. "It moved quickly, but we received the Bishop's blessing and purchased the building for $1 from the Diocese with the caveat that if it ceased to exist the property would go back to the Diocese of Fargo."

Colleen Samson explained, "We proceeded to move forward with the Bishop's recommendations. A board was established, and we worked and walked beside Mary Pat as she began this extremely difficult task of starting a local maternity home in Warsaw."

At this point, Father Richard LaCourt had invited Mary Pat and Colleen to share their idea with the community at Saint Stanislaus Catholic Church, despite Father Hils absence on sabbatical. While Saint Gianna's Maternity Home would eventually become instrumental in the fabric of the Warsaw community, at this time Mary Pat and the idea of a maternity home were foreign those in the area. Combined with the absence of their pastor, some in the Warsaw community had many questions when it came to the idea of a maternity home. Becoming part of the community in a small, rural town takes time. However, the pro-life mission of the Home attracted loyalty and support almost immediately.

"I remember Jason Plutowski came up to us after we spoke," shared Mary Pat. "He said that he and his family would help in any way that they could."

This conversation with Jason, who is still involved with the Home to this day, shows the generous spirit of the family of the Saint Gianna's Maternity Home since the beginning. The mission of the Maternity Home and the story of Saint Gianna tugs on the hearts of those who love life. The Home evokes a desire to share in the life-giving work. As people learned about the mission, it was not just a transaction of goods or money, but the building of a family that would welcome and love women and children.

Restoring Glory

"The building was in disrepair," recalled board member Joan Schanilec. "It was only partially finished when the Bethlehem Community was there. I distinctly remember, when we toured the building in the nineties, the graffiti on the walls all the way up to the top floor. The cement in the building heaved up really badly without any heating. It just sat and was unkempt. The building was a disaster."

The building was inhabitable at the time it was purchased and the question of whether it could be used was raised. An architect was hired to evaluate the property and make that judgment.

Despite the state of the building, many local people valued the rich history and Catholic presence that the building represented. Some of those involved with the volunteer work early on as well as a few of the earliest board members had personal ties to the old convent when it served the community as a school.

"We always saw it as holy ground," explained Joan Schanilec. "The kids who went to school there — many still in the area — are in their 70s and 80s now but the memories that they have are so special. So, we had the architect come and do a thorough examination of the building. He said, 'Well, the building will need a lot of work, but it has good bones.' And it was music to our ears, yet scary. It was the stamp to go ahead again. When you put it all together, God was orchestrating that: the way Father Hils asked Mary Pat about her plans at the retreat and the fact that Mary Pat said what she said; how Father Hils knew she should visit with Colleen Samson next — it was all directed by God and not a coincidence."

While the report from the architect was not dire, it presented a long list of needed renovations. The building was structurally sound but needed great improvements if it were to be suitable for mothers and children to live in it.

Father Hils, well versed in architecture, recalls the work needed to renovate the building. "All 64 windows had to be replaced as did all the doors. Inside we had to remove the 8x8 inch tiles that had been glued on the maple floors and refinish them. We had to remove fluorescent lights and plastic baseboards. We put in new baseboards to match the old ones and the new ones were encased in wood on the inside so they would match the existing wood casings from the rooms. We had to rip out false ceilings. As for the exterior, we had to tuck point the bricks and the bricks themselves needed attention. On top of the building, a small piece of flat roof needed to be replaced."

In addition to these repairs, the plumbing and electrical work would have to be brought up to code. Father Hils' expertise and appreciation of architecture ensured that the restoration of the building would honor its long history. Father Hils emphasized, "The restoration was historically sensitive and the whole place was restored to its original splendor. The building is a typical 1920s colonial-style home. In the 1920s the great innovation was that glass was mass-produced in larger proportions. Previously, glass was provided in small proportions with wood mullions — that would be more traditional colonial but the 1920s glass was mass-produced without the mullions. The Home has the proper windows for the period. There are no window panes because, in the 1920s, the bold statement was windows without the wood dividers. It was also common to have turrets — or towers — attached to the corner of the building, which you see with the Home."

In order to take in residents, the Maternity Home would also need to complete the necessary state licensing paperwork and file as a 501(c)3. The bylaws and legal forms to the insurance were necessary to open the doors of Saint Gianna's Maternity Home.

To complete renovations and meet legal requirements, the Home needed to acquire the necessary funds. While loans were an option, the board decided to trust in God's providence: the work would be completed as the funds were donated. Father Hils explained, "We never took out any loans and we never incurred any debt. We always paid our bills on time and that's why it took so long. We could have opened sooner if we had taken out loans, but we went a more conservative route and made sure we had the money."

This approach required great trust that God would provide the amount of money needed at the necessary time. Throughout the early stages of the Home, those involved could not look too far into the future. Instead, they leaned into the belief and trust that God would provide and make a way for its success in time.

It was not long before word spread through the Catholic world that a group of people were working to establish a maternity home in a small town in North Dakota. However, in the early days, the Home was still unnamed. Jean Eppler and Doreen Kennelly, teachers in the Fargo Catholic schools, wanted to donate in honor of their stepmother's passing. They asked Mary Pat who to write the check to.

"I was blessed to be able to choose Gianna," said Mary Pat. "It was Blessed Gianna at the time. When I was a teacher I always included her story as a beautiful and inspiring example of the holiness we are all called to."

It was this saintly wife and mother who inspired Mary Pat in her creation of the Maternity Home. Saint Gianna is known for her special care of women and children. Mary Pat sought to imitate her virtues that so beautifully affirmed the dignity of every human being.

Gianna Molla was beatified in the year 1994, with her husband, Pietro, and three remaining children present. When the Maternity Home began in 2001, Gianna's story was still in its early stages of being shared throughout the Church.

With the bishop's blessing and confidence in Blessed Gianna's example, the approval of an architect, and the small yet growing network of supporters, Mary Pat, Colleen, and Father Hils began the slow work of establishing what would become Saint Gianna's Maternity Home.

"It took much longer than I expected," said Mary Pat. "I remember I rented a house in Warsaw through December, thinking we would be ready, but we wouldn't open our doors until August of 2003."

God's blessing on the endeavor was evident despite the extra time needed to prepare the Home. Funding was secured to begin renovations and many generous people volunteered to help with the demolition and renovation work.

"We went to all these altar society meetings in every corner of North Dakota and Minnesota," said Mary Pat. "We asked them to be part of the mission. We chose Blessed Gianna at the right time because she wasn't that well known. When people heard about her, they fell in love with her story. She's a beautiful modern saint, had a happy marriage, was a doctor, and her sacrifice was for an unborn baby. People embraced our mission because of the inspiration of Gianna's life and her love and sacrifice."

Board member Joan Schanilec vividly recalled the spirit of the Board of Directors toward the finances of renovating the Home. "My prayer was 'Dear Jesus, if you want this to proceed, please keep opening doors and windows, but if you don't, please close doors and windows.'"

Doors and windows continued to open each step of the way, affirming the work and mission of the Maternity Home. Joan recalled a specific instance of God's providence in the process to update the Home to triple pane windows. Updating the windows was an instrumental step of the project, indicating if the building could retain heat as it stood or if much more extensive renovations than expected would be necessary.

"It was time to replace the windows," said Joan. "And we were able to strike a deal with Simonson Lumber and Marvin Windows at a reduced price, but it was still

$80,000. We had $1,300 in our account and we voted unanimously to proceed. By the time the windows came, we had all the money and more."

While it may seem foolish to some, voting to move ahead with the replacement demonstrated a strong commitment to trusting in God's plan to provide for the Home. Thanks to the generosity of many selfless donors, God's plan came to fruition. Through this act of faith, they were blessed not only with material answers but with graces to continue the work that was at hand.

"We've always had people step up," said Mary Pat. "People are pro-life, and they want to do something. This was something they could be a part of. This is one of the great things that Father Hils and other priests recommended — to get little supporters. In our newsletter, we list one founder, Father Hils, and he is. But we could also say that we have hundreds of founders — all who have donated money and become part of our family are our founders. Some have been donating monthly since the start."

As Mary Pat, Father Hils, and Colleen shared the story of Blessed Gianna and their dream for Blessed Gianna's Maternity Home, people started donating money. As people donated, they became a part of the Maternity Home family. They were not just participating in safeguarding and protecting life but also in building a family through which God's love could be shared.

"The Saint Gianna family is huge," said Mary Pat. "If we would have had a millionaire give us a bunch of money, it would have been easy. It would have seemed right and what we needed, but we wouldn't have what we have today. We have people who are loyal and faithful. We have people who are part of our family and a part of our work. It wasn't easy at the beginning, but we've got a big family and they care about us."

Once the building was deemed usable and funds continued to come in, the board grew, and the Home's mission was clarified. The board worked diligently and attended to new issues pertaining to the Home as they arose. Momentum continued to grow for the Maternity Home on the prairie and as it did, Mary Pat went to the new Bishop with hopes of being recognized as a Catholic apostolate.

On March 18, 2002, Archbishop Aquila (then Bishop) became Bishop of Fargo, succeeding Bishop Sullivan.

Archbishop Aquila

"When Mary Pat came to me and presented the vision of the Maternity Home, I was very receptive to it," recalled Archbishop Aquila. "Based on the dignity of human life and the unborn child, how do we promote the dignity of children and the gift of children? How do we help women who are in need? After she explained some of the needs of the Native American community and others in the Diocese of Fargo, I gave my full support."

Joining their mission to the mission of the Catholic Church, Blessed Gianna's Maternity Home sought to be established as a Catholic apostolate. Apostolate, coming from the word apostle, refers to the evangelical nature of a group or organization. Being deemed a Catholic apostolate recognizes the group or organization's desire to serve others and bring the life-saving message of Jesus to those it serves in accordance with the Catholic Church's teachings.

"Mary Pat spoke with me about the board and the mission of the apostolate," said Archbishop Aquila. "Then I issued a decree recognizing the apostolate as Catholic and one that deserved the support of the faithful."

Recalling the words of Saint John Paul II in his address to the world in preparation for the Jubilee Celebration, the Maternity Home was becoming an 'outward expression of the Church's rejoicing in salvation, creating conditions to ensure that the power of salvation may be shared by all.'

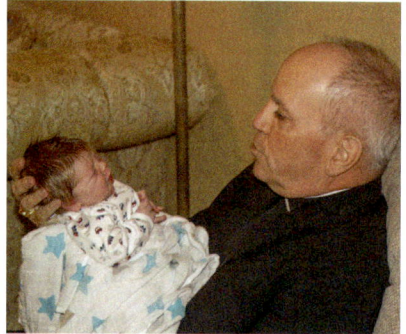

Archbishop Aquila with Thomas, one of our babies.

By recognizing Blessed Gianna's Maternity Home as a Catholic apostolate, Archbishop Aquila invited the faithful of the Diocese to be involved with the Home. He invited them to participate in its life-saving mission by donating money, volunteering, and praying for the women who would come to live there as well as those who would give their time to working with the women and children. Being established as an apostolate allowed the Maternity Home to be firmly rooted in the Diocese as an option for all women who might face an unexpected pregnancy or need an alternative to abortion.

"It has certainly reinforced for me how beautiful the pro-life mission is," remarked Archbishop Aquila. "And that the pro-life mission primarily needs to be a one-on-one relationship. They [volunteers, staff, Mary Pat] give tremendous witness to the gift of life but they also accompany the mother of the unborn child through the time of pregnancy and then, even beyond that, to make sure that they leave in a stable situation. It reinforces the Corporal Works of Mercy and how important they are in the promotion of human life."

The Beginning of the Beginning

After gathering support, organizing fundraisers, and collecting donations for nearly a year, it was time for physical work to begin in 2002.

Mary Pat, Father Hils, and Colleen turned to the Habitat for Humanity model to begin renovations. This model depends on volunteers offering their time and skills to build a home together. Those generously giving their time met on Saturdays after morning Mass and worked all day. Most of the renovations during the first eleven months were completed through the work of volunteers.

"I remember how nothing would happen all week and then 30-40 people would come on Saturday," said Mary Pat. "We'd have Mass and they'd work hard, and then we'd offer lunch and they'd go back and work until 4:00 p.m. or 5:00 p.m. I remember coming in on Saturday nights and being amazed by all the work that had been done in a day."

The work of the Maternity Home truly was a family effort. The volunteers came from near and far to be involved. Some traveled only a few miles down the road while others traveled over 90 miles to help with the renovations.

The renovations began with demolitions. In addition to taking out cosmetic and partial fixes that had been done over the years, the plumbing and electrical work had to be brought up to code in order to open.

"I remember the energy and the faith of the people who came on Saturdays," noted Father Hils. "Every Saturday families would come and they brought their children and their skills with them... They did all the work without complaint and we had lunch for them — that was all we could offer them. They worked in cold temperatures too; you could see their breath. They were so faithful."

Merlyn and Dolores Grabanski, lifetime residents of Warsaw, attended school in the Home when the building was a convent. They both made their first communions at the convent and decades later found themselves there alongside their son, Bryan, who was unrelenting in his support for the Maternity Home. He dedicated most of his Saturdays toward the renovation work in addition to giving generously of his money and prayers.

Bryan Grabanski

"After Bryan got involved with the renovation work on Saturdays, we started helping, too," shared Dolores. "He was a man of deep faith. He attended daily mass whenever he could, and he was on the board for the Home right away."

The Grabanski's were involved with both the exterior work on the property and the interior work. "We started by taking out the bushes south of the building," said Merlyn. "That was our son Bryan, Harold Grabanski, and me. We'd get together and pull out the bushes and haul them away. That was the beginning of the beginning."

Merlyn and Dolores Grabanski

"Merlyn laid all the floor tiles," explained Dolores. "I did staining and varnishing. We were pretty involved, and it turned out beautifully."

Dolores was also involved with the Saturday meals, and she has fond memories of her experience coordinating and helping serve the volunteers.

"One thing that I did early on was for the volunteers," said Dolores. "We served lunch on Saturdays for the men. We served a hot meal. Dina Muggli would coordinate the workers and would inform me how many were coming, and I organized the cooks. I'd call women and ask them if they would be willing to serve a meal. They would plan their menu, provide the food, cook it, and provide paper plates and cups. They would also clean up after serving. And the response was very good. I had women that came from Warsaw, Veseleyville, Grafton, Drayton, Grand Forks, and East Grand Forks. Meals included spaghetti, lasagna, turkey and dressing, meatballs, beef stew...the workers were very appreciative. Some of the men jokingly said they came for the meal."

From the 'beginning of the beginning,' the spirit of hospitality exemplified in the life of Saint Gianna was mirrored through the Home. As volunteers came to share their time and talent, the only adequate response was to give back to them. This took the form of prayers and food.

Imitating its patroness, the Maternity Home established a rule of generosity from the start. This rule extended not only to the women and children who would come to live at the Home but also to anyone who would encounter the Home. Seeing God provide for them over and over, Mary Pat and the board could only take up the highest measure of generosity knowing that God would always provide for their needs.

"I think that the kindness and the welcoming spirit of Saint Gianna lives on in Warsaw," said Father Hils. "She was a very kind and gracious doctor. The ladies who came to her for help — she was so kind and generous to them. She wasn't in it for the money. She was in it to help people, and that's the spirit of Saint Gianna's Maternity Home."

Despite the increasing momentum regarding the mission of the Home, many people still questioned the efforts being made to renovate the old convent. The work seemed like a meager attempt by a small group of people because the work was slow and occurred in bursts on Saturdays. The building was located 30 miles away from Grand Forks, the nearest reasonably-sized town. Some believed that the project had no chance at success.

Bryan Grabanski working outside Saint Stanislaus Church.

Volunteer and board member, Bryan Grabanski, never shied from defending the work to the skeptics. Bryan was deeply connected to the life of the Church and the pro-life movement. In response to those questioning the process of creating a maternity home, Bryan simply said, "If we save even one baby, it will have been worth all the work."

Bryan Grabanski's words capture the heart of the mission at Saint Gianna and Pietro Molla's maternity home. Each life deserves respect and a child deserves a chance. The Home's mission does not involve changing the whole world overnight. However, the Home's work can change the life of one woman and her child, making all the sacrifices worthwhile.

It's about loving one baby, one mother, one family at a time.

Bryan's role as a volunteer led him to joining the original board at the Maternity Home. He held this position until his premature death in 2005.

"He got to see that first baby — the one baby to make it all worth it," said Dolores referring to Geianna Meade, the first baby born, whose birthday is October 22, 2004.

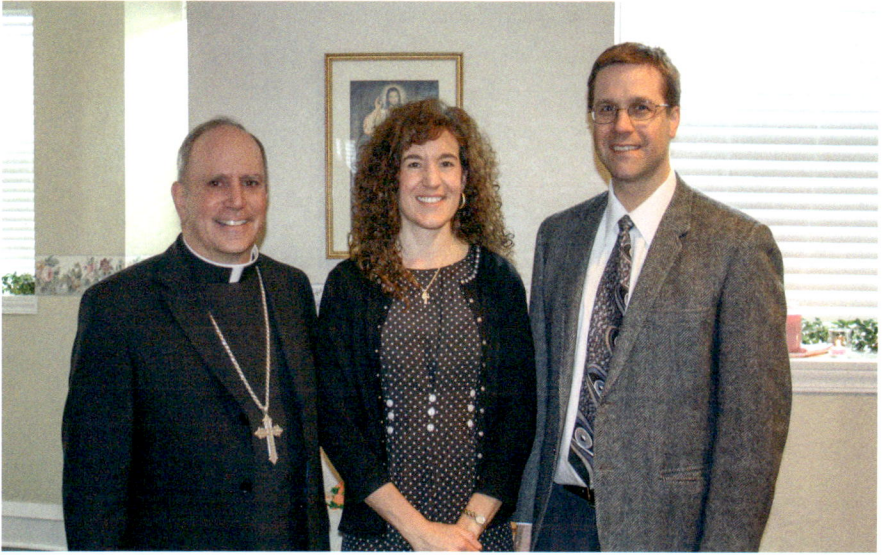

Archbishop Aquila with Dina & Darrin Muggli.

Helping Hands

Engineers Dina and Darren Muggli volunteered their expertise and time to organize the renovation of the Home.

Mary Pat gratefully expressed, "Their time and talent was absolutely invaluable in the renovation work. We will always be indebted to the great generosity of their family."

Dina, writing for one of the earliest issues of the Maternity Home newsletter, shared an update showing how many people were generously involved to make the doors open:

> Because of the limited funding currently available, the board of directors elected to utilize volunteers instead of hiring contractors to expedite the renovation. We've proposed executing the renovation following the model of Habitat for Humanity, in which representatives from the construction trades volunteer their expertise in their respective fields (electrical, plumbing, heating, and air conditioning, etc.) and volunteers perform the work with donated materials or materials procured at cost.

The response within the Grand Forks and surrounding Walsh County community has been overwhelming! Rick Simonson, of Simonson Lumber, Grafton, provided energy-efficient Marvin Windows at cost. Dan Syrup, of Strata Concrete, Grand Forks, donated all the concrete necessary to pour new sidewalks, gravel for the parking lot, and equipment as needed. Dennis Markesen, of Walsh County, donated sand and black dirt for the external renovation work, and Roger Feltman, of Warsaw, donated dirt and equipment.

Phil Kraemer, with Lunseth Plumbing, Grand Forks, is leading the plumbing effort, and Lunseth Plumbing is donating laborers and most of the materials to complete the plumbing upgrades. Paul Samson, of Samson Electric, Park River, is heading the electrical phase of the project and is donating substantial labor and materials to complete the electrical renovation.[7]

A great supporter of the project was Roger Feltman, a native of Warsaw, ND. He was born and raised in the town and always attended church at Saint Stanislaus with his family. Roger attended school for eight years at the convent which would later become the Maternity Home. Together with his father and brothers, Roger worked in farming and carpentry. His involvement with the Home started when volunteers were first needed and continued for over 20 years.

Roger recalled, "After Father Hils and Mary Pat got together and made the board, they asked for volunteers. I volunteered to work with Father Hils in the Chapel area. I wanted to leave it exactly the way it was when the sisters were there, and it was very important for the four windows up front to be left — they were donated by Sisters and their families wanted them remembered. It was kind of funny when I went into the Chapel with Father Hils. He said, 'Do you want to go first or should I?' So he went through and explained how he wanted to do this and do that and he finally got done and he said, 'Now, what's your plan?' I said, 'Ah, yours is good.' It was a little different than the way it was before, but it was good."

Roger fondly remembered the Chapel when the convent was open. The two sides of the pews extended from the front all the way to the back. The sacristy was divided into two rooms — one for the confessional and one for the sacristy with all the vestments. The Mother Superior's office was located where the current confessional is, and there was a door to it where the mechanical room now is. The office today is where the formal living room was and to the northwest corner, where the guest room is, the formal dining room was located.

"My dad built the altars," said Roger. "He built them out of scratch. We cleaned it up, and it looks awesome now."

Roger proudly referred to the Chapel work as a "father-son project". His expertise in carpentry helped the Home open sooner and his generous donation of his labor brought costs of renovation down greatly.

"They wanted to strip all the woodwork down and re-stain it," said Roger. "The bid was high to strip every door and baseboard. I visited with them and I asked if we could try sanding them lightly, staining them, and putting a lacquer over them. I tried a little piece, and they liked it, and we were able to save maybe $10,000 or more."

For many like Roger, it was important to restore the building to its former glory when it served as a convent and school and honor the historical integrity of the building. The rich history of the building is honored through the Maternity Home's mission and operation. Roger expressed this preservation by explaining, "The building was getting dilapidated. But now it looks awesome — everything is clean and neat; everything is preserved."

Roger is a lifelong Catholic who has great memories of serving at the altar, especially at the Good Friday services that took place at midnight when he was a young boy. The presence of the Home has deepened his faith and given him hope.

"I just hope that we can keep it going," said Roger. "If it can keep going and make a little impression on some of the people that are not quite pro-life, that makes a difference. We just look at the girls at the Home, but there's a whole lot more that goes on with the pro-life cause. My son and his wife were having a hard time having children. She called Mary Pat who sent a rosary with a Saint Gianna medal and prayers to her. Within three months they were expecting their first child, and now they have four boys. It's good to know there are places like the Maternity Home out there."

Recalling the generosity that makes the running of the Home possible, Roger said, "Everybody helped quite a bit. I think if they ever need anything, there wouldn't be a problem. People donate and there's Giving Hearts Day, and they always make their goal. They have a lot of donors from far away, too. I think it makes a difference here, and that it makes a difference everywhere."

Roger, along with those involved in the project, knew there was great meaning behind his efforts. "The most rewarding part is if we can save them kids. Bryan Grabanski was my first cousin, and some people would be complaining a little bit about how much it was going to cost, and it would cost quite a bit, and he said if we can save just one, it will be worth it."

As this book goes to print, Roger has passed to his eternal reward. (2/12/2024) He was a dear friend, neighbor, and supporter. His help and friendship will never be forgotten. May he rest in peace.

Roger Feltman, September 2022.

Phil and Laurie Kraemer have been longtime residents of Grand Forks and members of Saint Michael's Catholic Church. When renovations first began for the Maternity Home, the Kraemer's had five children and had been longtime advocates for the pro-life movement. They attended the informational meeting about the Home that was held at their parish.

"We were at the very first meeting that Mary Pat and Father Hils had at Saint Michael's," recalled Laurie. "They shared their vision and what they hoped to do, and we were very excited. I said that I had a 4-H club that would like to do things and help. Mary Pat called me up, and we were the very first volunteer group to do something. Our Eagles 4-H club went up and planted tulips. I think the tulips were a little premature because I think most of them were excavated but maybe a few survived. Mary Pat wanted everything to be beautiful — inside and out."

Helping out with the renovations for Saint Gianna's Maternity Home became a part of the Kraemer's family life during this time. While unfamiliar with the story of Saint Gianna before they learned of the Maternity Home, the Kraemers "became pretty familiar with her fairly quickly." The older four of their five children (including now Father Kraemer and Seminarian Tim Kraemer) joined in the demolition and cleaning in Warsaw.

Laurie Kraemer said, "The next stage was when we started helping during the Saturday work days. The boys really enjoyed that. Peter and Timothy did demolition work. Sarah and I triple-washed the walls. It seemed endless, but it was good because you were working with other people."

"There was a lot of demo work," shared Phil. "There was a lot of lath and plaster to come down, a lot of things behind walls — electrical, plumbing, mechanical — it was a lot of discovery and figuring out as you go. We had enough people who were willing to share their expertise. They would come and look around and give their recommendations. Not all of the people who helped shared just sweat equity. People came and shared their expertise and that helped tremendously."

Phil, who works as Vice President of Operations at Lunseth's, helped not only with sweat, equity, and expertise but also by inviting his workplace to contribute.

"I twisted some arms at the office," said Phil. "It wasn't free, but we were able to offer a very reduced cost. Jim Kasprick, a fellow employee at Lunseth's, is from the Minto area and was able to watch over the project. His experience over the years helped make things flow. There are challenges with an old building like that, to make everything work, and it took a few years of redoing things to make everything up to code."

Years later, Phil and Laurie's love for and involvement with the Maternity Home would come full circle when their daughter and son-in-law, Matthew and Sarah Komprood, adopted their daughter from one of the residents at the Maternity Home.

Laurie shared, "The most significant thing for us has been Ella's [Emanuela's] adoption. To meet the birth mother and birth grandparents, to receive a granddaughter through adoption – it's unbelievable. Who would have ever thought that would be the 'coming around' moment for us? The Lord always blesses you, but that was the ultimate blessing – to bring a child into our family through adoption."

"It was totally unexpected," agreed Phil. "But when you look back, you see that that's how God works."

Alongside Lunseth's Plumbing and Heating, Samson Electric of Park River was involved with the electrical work from the beginning. Paul Samson, Colleen Samson's husband, was the manager-owner of Samson Electric and found their involvement with the Home's renovations to be a unique but worthwhile experience.

"It was very rewarding to work alongside the design team and the armies of volunteers," said Paul. "It was also very gratifying to see the end product completed and to see the mission of the Home continue to go forward."

Samson Electric donated its labor for the project and was honored to be able to do the electrical construction for the Home as well.

"In addition, Paul contacted one of his main electrical material suppliers, Dakota Supply Group, to ask for their involvement," said Colleen. "They were graciously willing to donate a lot of the materials needed. The Home was wired for a fraction of the cost it would normally take to wire a building of this magnitude. The Samson Electric employees received many blessings by participating in the wiring of the Home."

The Maternity Home is the result of many people bringing their God-given gifts to the table. Many involved in the work experienced for the first time an opportunity to put action to their convictions. The work of the Maternity Home has invited countless people over the years to experience what it means to be pro-life first hand. Many are often surprised by what they find — that living out the pro-life mission isn't just about protecting unborn babies, but also honoring and cherishing life in all its stages.

Saint Gianna herself was an example of this love as she deeply embraced life in its many stages prior to becoming a wife and mother. Her life exhibited the great joy of life that comes when you recognize Christ in each person. It is a daily task that God calls all to take up.

After spending two years fundraising, renovating the Home, and getting the proper licensing to take in women and children, Blessed Gianna's Maternity Home had a small celebration with the Board of Directors. It took place on August 15, 2003, the Feast of the Assumption. The next day, August 16, 2003, was the grand opening of Blessed Gianna's Maternity Home, with almost 900 in attendance.

August 26, 2003 Archbishop Aquila lights the lamp outside our Home on our grand opening day with the assistance of Phil Kraemer.

Therese Warmus attended the public celebration and shared her reflections on the opening at the time.

"Saturday, August 16th, dawned hot and humid. Holy Mass marking the dedication of the new Blessed Gianna's Maternity Home and the blessing of the new altar in Saint Stanislaus Church would not begin until 10:30 a.m., yet attendees were already arriving by 7:30 a.m. when I pulled up in the parking lot behind the 'Cathedral of the Prairie.'

The Catholic parish in Warsaw has an unusual congregation. The list of 'regulars' is modest, but their reputation for reverence in all things sacred, particularly the Eucharist, is well known, and on any given feast you may find the church filled to the rafters with the faithful from as far away as New York City. This day would be no exception.

On my last visit to the new Maternity Home, there had been drywall dust and workmen still framing interior walls, the debris of reconstruction everywhere. Now the floors were brilliantly polished. I pulled off my shoes and looked around. The old convent seemed new, and mansion-like, its massive woodwork giving it the air of distinction, yet the place already had that warm, lived-in feeling that no palace can match, no matter how grand.

In a house of well-proportioned rooms, it is difficult to pick one as most lovely, but the chapel would triumph in any contest. Upon entering, the visitor's eye is arrested by the beautiful backdrop behind the altar of repose: The Visitation of Mary to Elizabeth, in vivid coloring. On the right wall, Blessed Gianna Beretta Molla ascends to Heaven under the welcoming eye of Our Lady Herself.

I was pleased to see that the chapel's stained glass windows were retained intact, as they originally stood when the convent was built. A shrine to Saint Gerard Majella, patron of expectant mothers, stood at the entrance of the confessional. The inclusion of a chapel is a European tradition in the stately homes of Catholic nobility; it seemed very natural here, and in line with the Home's former status as a religious house.

There was no time to linger though, and I finished my round practically at a run.

Ten o'clock, and inside Saint Stanislaus Church the pews were already filling. I found a seat somewhere in the middle of the activity and settled in. As the time to begin Mass neared, I was surprised to see so many young children, especially babies in the arms of their mothers and fathers. Space was at a premium; the church was already full to capacity, and more waited to be seated. With that many people in the building, it was bound to be warm, and it certainly was.

The choir, gathered from surrounding parishes, sang glorious hymns, accompanied by organ and flute. I sat riveted by sight and sound, nearly melting in the intense heat, and would not have traded my spot for a cool drink of water. Time indeed stood still and yet flew.

Outside afterward, I ran across a young man I knew rather well. He introduced me to his beautiful sister, a young single mother with one small daughter. 'She just wants to help in any way she can,' he said. Her happiness shone through her eyes, and she seemed to embody every woman I met that day.

A large open-air tent was set up just outside with long tables and comfortable chairs for lunch, and nearly everyone who attended ate the wonderful food. At 1:30 p.m. the official entertainment began: The Polish National Alliance Dancers gave a number of exhibitions of the unique form of folk dancing they are famous for, all the more amazing was their stamina in the oppressive weather. Graced with beribboned headdresses, brightly colored costumes, and high-top shoes, girls of all ages spun and swirled their way through polkas, marches, and even a waltz, their male partners likewise handsomely attired.

It became difficult to remain still in the presence of such joyful strains and perhaps for the first time, I, an American of German extraction, began to understand why Polish music is such a mainstay at weddings in this area, even among non-Poles.

A young man with a camera briefly joined us under our little tree — shade is rare in Warsaw — and remarked that at one time his younger brother had been a dancer in this troupe. 'You feel rather stupid as a boy, all dressed up like that,' he said; but his eyes betrayed enjoyment. His feet, too, were tapping with the music.

Later some 600 visitors had passed through the Home, I collapsed, exhausted, on the wide cement steps outside. A middle-aged woman was sitting there; she had related to me earlier something of her life story, a teenage pregnancy, the divorce that followed a hasty marriage, and the struggle to make ends meet alone. We gazed up at the roof of Saint Stanislaus across the road and then at the little grotto that adorns the grounds of the Maternity Home. 'It's a miracle, isn't it?' she said finally."[8]

After a marathon of fundraising, paperwork, demolition, and renovations spanning years, Blessed Gianna's Maternity Home opened its doors and could finally begin the real work: sharing Christ's joy, peace, and love with women in crisis pregnancy situations.

Father Joseph holds three of our little ones: Caliona, Luca, and Aubrey.

Unexpected Answers to Prayers and the Franciscan Spirit

The first few years of the Maternity Home were filled with slow and steady work, trial and error, and renewed trust in God's providence. Throughout those early years, a frequent prayer request was for God to bring an order of religious Sisters to the Maternity Home. The work of the Home happened at all hours of the day and night, and for a long time, the "perfect" plan was for a group of women dedicated to the Lord to take over the mission of the Home.

From the Sisters of Life on the East Coast to the Servants of the Plan of God in Peru, various religious sisters came to the Maternity Home in the first few years. Yet, none returned to take up the work as a part of their order's formal mission.

Father Hils would move back to Kentucky in the summer of 2007. While nobody could have expected this transition ahead of time, God already had the perfect plan in place, once again revealing His care for Saint Gianna's Maternity Home.

Upon leaving, Father Hils told Mary Pat to contact Father Joseph Christensen, a Franciscan of Mary Immaculate (FMI) and friend from the seminary also stationed in the Fargo Diocese.

"Father Hils and I graduated from seminary together," said Father Joseph. "We met in the dining hall on graduation day, and we would always try to go to our classmates' ordinations if we could, but for Father Hils – I had no idea where Fargo was. I just knew it was way out west. We were in seminary on the East Coast, and I was familiar with Michigan but Fargo was still 1,000 miles from there. I remember I shook his hand and I said, 'All the best, you'll be in my prayers.' I was wishing him well, but in my head I was thinking 'I don't know if I'll ever see you again.' So, God has a sense of humor."

Father Hils and Father Joseph had this exchange in 1995, well before the inception of the Maternity Home, but not before God was planning and preparing for this special Home on the Prairie.

Father Joseph's path to the Maternity Home was one ordained by God alone. After finishing seminary in 1995, Father Joseph's heart was prepared for religious life with the Franciscan Friars stationed in Michigan. By August of 1996, that community had moved to the Fargo Diocese, taking up residence just down the road from Warsaw in Pisek. Father Joseph was ordained a Franciscan priest on May 31, 1997.

A few years later in 2001, the Franciscan order was dissolved and Father Joseph

> "Here is something right in our backyard that is pro-life and concrete and so I should say *yes*."

returned to a friary in Michigan until Bishop Aquila called him back to the Fargo Diocese in 2003.

"When the Home opened, I was at Saint Joseph's in Devils Lake," said Father Joseph. "Father Wilhelm came to the opening but I didn't. I had heard about it and read about it when it was being remodeled. I was in Devils Lake for three and a half years and then moved to Saints Anne and Joachim in Fargo from 2006 to 2007. Father Hils told Mary Pat when he was leaving to call Father Joseph and tell him about her spiritual needs because he won't refuse her. Mary Pat called me and I asked her a lot of questions about how often to come and what was expected. When I hung up the phone I immediately thought, before doing anything else, here is something right in our backyard that is pro-life and concrete and so I should say yes. That was immediate."

Beginning in the fall of 2007, Father Joseph began offering monthly days of recollection for the staff and board at Saint Gianna's. Marked by a Franciscan love for the beauty of creation and life itself, Father Joseph brought spiritual encouragement, the joy of Christ, and prayer with him as he began ministering to the staff, residents, and community in this small prairie town.

Aubrey assisting Father Joseph with lighting the candles before Mass.

From 2007 to 2011 Father Joseph continued offering days of recollection with greater frequency while also being stationed at the Cathedral of Saint Mary's in Fargo. He became the spiritual director of the Home, and as his work at the Home intertwined with another stirring of the Spirit: his desire to live a religious life in the community.

In 2009, Father Joseph met with Bishop Aquila, with the intention of sharing his desire to move back into religious life from his work as a diocesan priest. Prepared to act in obedience to his Bishop, Father Joseph was delighted to receive Bishop Aquila's blessing to discern his return to religious life.

"I just felt very called to the way of life I had lived with the Franciscans," said Father Joseph. "Bishop Aquila had me come up with a 5-year business plan for starting a Franciscan Order in the Diocese of Fargo. It was good and opened my eyes to what I needed to do."

Alongside this confidential work of discernment, Father Joseph continued to minister to those at Saint Gianna's Maternity Home. It was a moment in prayer that gave Father Joseph clarity in what God wanted him to do.

"I was praying during a Holy Hour and it came to me," said Father Joseph. "It was like a sign flipping down saying for the friary to be here [in Warsaw]. First, to be physically close to the Home. Secondly, Warsaw is Polish and our community has Polish customs and traditions; I can help with the parish. Third, it's a country setting. It's a small town in the country but still convenient for shopping or travel in Grafton and Grand Forks."

On May 31, 2011, the Third Order Franciscans of Mary Immaculate was established as an official Religious Community of the Diocese of Fargo, settled in the community of Warsaw. The Franciscans of Mary Immaculate live out their religious life of prayer, chastity, and obedience in Warsaw, allowing Father Joseph to remain spiritual director and chaplain for Saint Gianna's and assist in the local parish of Saint Stanislaus.

May 11, 2015. Gianna Emanuela's first visit to our Home in Warsaw.

Of the relationship between the Franciscan Friary and the Maternity Home, Father Joseph said, "You can't build a relationship if you're not ever here, but it has worked out pretty nice because the residents can get to know us, too, and there's interaction. If it's all women here, it's good to have a balance and have men coming in and hopefully good men, good examples and offer a balance to their life and to ours, too. From that relationship is where you can help build them up with human formation to whatever extent we would be an example. Or we can build them up in our speech and then the next step is building them up in the faith and teaching the faith."

In countless ways, the life and work of the Franciscans, most importantly Father Joseph, stands as a testament of faith for the residents who come to Saint Gianna's. They offer the experience of fatherly and brotherly love that many do not experience. Having

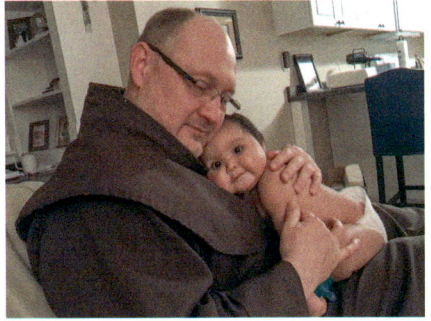

Father Joseph holding one of his godchildren.

become godfathers, role models, and helping hands, Father Joseph has provided a paternal aspect to the love of God experienced by the residents and staff at the Home.

On a Mission

From its inception, the Maternity Home has protected the God-given right to life from natural conception until natural death. In a culture that often attacks the dignity of the human person and tells women that abortion is the perfect solution for an unexpected pregnancy, the Maternity Home combats these lies with the individualized love and care they show each woman and child.

The Maternity Home's mission statement guides the daily life of the women and children served at the Home. The mission statement only begins to scratch the surface of the great acts of love present at this maternity home. Here is the statement in its entirety:

We believe that every unborn child has a right to life and that every pregnant woman has the right to give birth with dignity. We are dedicated to providing safe shelter, food, clothing, education, and counseling; and to address the physical, emotional, and spiritual needs of women in crisis pregnancies as an alternative to abortion. We are committed to providing families with a stable living situation based on spiritual values — one mother, one baby, one family at a time.

We believe that every unborn child has a right to life and that every pregnant woman has the right to give birth with dignity.

The pro-life movement in our country is wrongly portrayed as focusing solely on the unborn children. To villainize pro-life efforts, abortion advocates claim that the pro-life cause views mothers as expendable and less important than their unborn children. This pro-abortion culture labels abortion as a battle over women's 'rights,' declaring the pro-life stance as demeaning for women and abortion as the epitome of a woman's freedom. While the battle to provide alternatives to abortion is about saving the unborn, a comprehensive pro-life stance is impossible without including the mothers. For each unborn baby threatened by abortion, there is also a woman in need. Oftentimes this woman can believe the isolating lie that she is too weak and unprepared to be a mother, buying into the pro-choice lie that feeds the abortion industry and seeks to destroy the family.

The first sentence of Saint Gianna's mission statement combats the culture of death by declaring the right to life for each unborn child and the right for each pregnant woman to give birth with dignity. The Home serves the unborn and pregnant women together, precisely because it is impossible to be pro-life and turn away from helping mothers.

Each woman who lives at Saint Gianna's Maternity Home finds that the goal is not simply to bring new life into the world. The Home provides women with an opportunity to give birth with dignity. It is an invitation to a better life. This looks different for each woman and family who reside at the Home, but commonality exists in showing women the beauty and goodness in making a family and Christ's merciful love for everyone who turns to Him.

> "Saint Gianna's Maternity Home stands in the face of a troubled culture and declares that *God's gift of life is beautiful.*"

The pro-life worldview transcends the matter of abortion. It is a joyful embrace of the life God has made – even with suffering, poverty, and hardship. Living out the pro-life message is a remarkable affirmation of the goodness present in life that comes from a good God. This countercultural message finds meaning in Christ, as the sufferings in this world are united to His own suffering on the Cross.

Saint Gianna's Maternity Home stands in the face of a troubled culture and declares that God's gift of life is beautiful, and Christ redeems all suffering. Those who encounter the Home are invited to experience how God's love reaches into human brokenness and makes the person whole through mercy and healing. Father Joseph explains this in the way the staff offer the love of Christ to the residents:

> What comes first is that they love these women, which then translates into or equals that they care for them. They form them, teach them, and help them. They feed them, clothe them, shelter them, and recreate with them. A lot of the residents struggle with trust and authority because the authority or adults in their lives have failed them. So, the work of the Home is building them up and showing them that it is possible to trust people; that it is possible to love. It's not just information or just forming them. It's like a family – it's what you do to a child, you help them in all aspects of their lives. It's human formation and faith formation and everything in between.

Saint Gianna's Maternity Home is an invitation to view life as God sees it: precious and worthy of dignity. By embodying this ideal in the world, it crosses lines of politics and denominations, and challenges others to see that life is the greatest gift.

We are dedicated to providing safe shelter, food, clothing, education, and counseling; and to addressing the physical, emotional, and spiritual needs of women in crisis pregnancies as an alternative to abortion.

The next part of the mission statement outlines the offerings of the Maternity Home in providing the necessities entitled to each person, precisely because they are precious in the eyes of God.

"I think that every maternity home is unique," said Mary Pat Jahner. "We are unique in our strong Catholic identity. We have a chapel and the sacraments. We have live-in staff and we live as a family with the women and children we serve. We eat meals together, pray together, work together and enjoy leisure time together as well "

Saint Gianna's Maternity Home is unique in its individualized care for each woman. The formation provided by the Home encompasses their physical, emotional, educational, and spiritual needs.

When women choose to move to Saint Gianna's Maternity Home, they choose to change their past lifestyles. They move to a rural home that offers an opportunity to retreat from busyness and experience the peace that only God can give. "There is a lot of chaos in the world," Mary Pat reflected. "We protect the people who come here — that is our first focus, to maintain the family we have here."

The vision for Saint Gianna's Maternity Home is to treat the whole person — body, mind, and soul. Each woman who resides at the Home is treated individually. The needs vary greatly from woman to woman, but the bottom line is the same: Saint Gianna's serves its residents as a Catholic Home of formation. Each woman is treated with dignity and respect; this is the integral aspect of serving in imitation of Saint Gianna. Many women who find themselves in crisis pregnancies have experienced difficult family situations, struggles with abuse, drugs, and alcohol, or other unfortunate circumstances. The beginning of formation at the Maternity Home is reminding these daughters of Christ that nothing has the power to take away their dignity and human worth.

"What I see as the philosophy of the Home is the emphasis that the Home always puts on the value of the lives of the women, the life of the child — unborn or the one she brings with her," said Joan Schanilec. "A lot of women have been so hurt, wounded, abused physically, emotionally or sexually. Some women come with only one plastic grocery bag of things — either because that's all they had or they had to leave in a hurry. They come and we treat each woman how Christ would treat them."

When a woman comes to live at the Home, they become incorporated into the life of a family. They experience the fullness of a new community through joining in the spiritual life of the Home with Mass and daily prayers, taking part in household chores and cooking, learning how to do laundry and care for children, and completing their education through high school or college coursework. Other women work on skills training or earn their driver's license.

"It takes a lot of hours and effort to do the work," said Father Joseph. "It's helping someone who's been broken or down and out or afraid and hurt. The work here is where the rubber meets the road. It's the nitty-gritty." This family model with emphasis on individualized care is what makes the Saint Gianna and Pietro Molla Maternity Home special and effective. In order for the Home to operate, each member must do their part as an individual for the betterment of the whole family unit, and this is accomplished most perfectly when it is done out of love for others.

We are committed to providing families with a stable living situation based on spiritual values.

"I think the philosophy of the Home — the vision — is to love the women who come here," said Mary Pat Jahner. "We have the Visitation Chapel and the words above the tabernacle are, 'the child in my womb leapt for joy.' When do we feel joy in life? It is when we feel loved — by God and by others. The chapel is the heart of our Home, and that is our work — to bring joy to their lives, especially while they are experiencing a chaotic time or a sad time. We want them to feel love and joy."

At its core, the top priority of the Saint Gianna Maternity Home is to create an environment where all who live there experience Christ's love.

This is experienced through the many ways that the Catholic faith permeates the schedule at the Home. The residents participate in prayers before meals and at night and attend Mass on Sunday. By designing the Home around the Eucharistic presence of Christ in the Tabernacle, the Home invites women to withdraw from their normal routines and begin again. It invites them to face the restlessness and hardship in their lives in a sacred space where they can open their hearts to Christ's love and peace and hopefully accept mercy and healing. The vision for the Home is to provide an opportunity for women to encounter this love and carry it with them for the rest of their lives, in suffering and in joy.

"

"The Home is to provide an opportunity for women to *encounter this love* and carry it with them for the rest of their lives, in suffering and in joy."

The presence of Christ in the Tabernacle at the Home is a tangible offering of peace, and the family life based on communion, further welcomes Christ's presence by inviting the women to experience God through the love and service of those around them every day.

For Joan Schanilec, the following quote from Saint Teresa of Avila beautifully describes the work of the home:

> Christ has no body on earth but yours; yours are the only hands with which He can do His work; yours are the only feet with which He can go about the world; yours are the only eyes through which His compassion can shine forth upon a troubled world. Christ has no body on earth but yours.

"This is what I see lived out at the Home all the time," said Joan. "It is Christ at work. Through that home, through Mary Pat the Director, through the housemothers, the women, the donors, the adoptive parents — it's Christ at work in that home. As you have done unto others, you have done unto me. This isn't just a flash in the pan; it is a consistent belief system — day after day, month after month, year after year, to teach women about self-worth."

One Baby, One Mother, One Family at a Time

The mission of Saint Gianna's Maternity Home will always be one of helping one baby, one mother, and one family at a time. Each resident of the Home does not become a mere number or statistic but is seen for who they are as an individual. As the years unfolded, Mary Pat saw that the goal was not a constant increase in the numbers of women living at the Home, but to learn the best ways to serve the women who are already in residence there.

"We're always evolving," said Mary Pat. "We're not changing the mission, but we're learning what's important and learning what's not important. We take people where they're at, and we're small, so we're able to provide more individualized care. In the beginning, I think I had loftier goals, but if women can grow a little in faith, a little in education, and a little emotionally, then that is what we can consider small victories. I used to think we needed to be able to solve each woman's problems. But, I've learned that we really just need to show them true love and compassion and meet them where they are in life. We accomplish that in working together with them on little goals each day and everything else we entrust to the Lord."

This dedication to provide a stable living environment and individualized care allows the Home to forever change the lives of the women who call Saint Gianna's "home."

A Flagship for Life

Without fail, God has continued to bless Saint Gianna's Maternity Home and all those who find their lives intertwined with the life of the Home. Guided by this mission statement, the Home has become a 'flagship' guiding countless people to embrace the Gospel of Life in a deeper way, as shared by Father Joseph:

> People want to help. They want to do something for the pro-life movement. What can you actually or concretely do? You can go to the abortion facility and pray or you can donate, but they want to be doing something more, and here there is something happening. I really believe that this is a flagship to remind people of the necessity for it and a reminder of the pro-life mindset. We need each benefactor, each person who donates to help fulfill the mission; otherwise, we can't do what we do. We're grateful, and we pray for them daily.

Board President Colleen Samson echoes these sentiments as she reflects on the work:

> When I see the many women, men, and children that have been touched by Mary Pat, the staff and volunteers as well as board members, and Father Joseph, the Spiritual Father of the Home, I see the fruits of their years of labor and love. Truly God has ordained this pro-life ministry to help all of us on our spiritual journey to eternity. This beacon of light has shown many the path to truth and encouraged us to make our world a better place to live and serve others.

The Saint Gianna and Pietro Molla Maternity Home – a beacon of light – illuminates the lives of all who encounter it. The secret behind its service lies in the fact that when a woman or child walks through the doors, they are welcomed with open arms into a family with love beyond comparison.

"
"When a woman or child walks through the doors, they are *welcomed with open arms* into a family with love beyond comparison."

Board of Directors

The Board of Directors at Saint Gianna's Maternity Home serves as a working board, brainstorming and problem solving as well as working directly with the housemothers and residents to complete tasks and help manage the Home. In the beginning years, this looked like forming ground rules, filing the appropriate paperwork, and assisting with grants, policies, and fundraisers. As time has gone on, the board has served a vital role in supporting the women and children who become residents at the Home.

Patricia Traynor, moard member from 2004 to 2007, recalls her experience: "We had to get the state to sign off on the building, meet the requirements for the licensing, and help solve whatever problems emerged. We had a strong feeling for the mission of the Home, a belief in its need, and a commitment to its purpose. We were dealing with things in the moment. Of course, we were planning and looking to the future, but there was a feeling that God would provide and we didn't have to solve everything. We just needed to take care of what needed to be done that month."

As residents arrived and licensing and paperwork became familiar, the board members became integral to the functioning of the Home. At times, these Directors assist by transporting residents to appointments, helping with the children, and inviting the residents into their homes to experience family life. These unique facets of being a board member of the Home accompany the usual tasks of planning events, fundraising, or contacting donors. While the board serves as the governing body, helping to make decisions on the future of the Home, the members of the board become friendly faces to the residents and a part of their broader community.

Eleri Kerian, board member since 2009, moved to North Dakota with her husband James Kerian, and was immediately drawn to the life of the Home.

"I began to volunteer at the Home when I was pregnant with my second child in 2008," said Eleri. "I tutored residents, spent time doing crafts with them, and our little family would occasionally come over and be 'on duty' for a while so the housemothers could have a meeting or go out. It was a blessing to be able to get to know and care for several residents and their children this way."

Though a young, busy mother herself, Eleri recognized the need to put actions behind her pro-life beliefs.

"It has always been important to me to be involved in the servant side of the pro-life movement," said Eleri. "It takes all kinds of people to help protect the unborn: lobbyists, prayer warriors, benefactors, and volunteers who are willing to help meet even the most basic needs for our families."

Eventually, Eleri would become a board member, sharing her talents and heart with the Home in this way.

"We refer to our board as a working board," said Eleri. "We meet regularly to address the needs of the Home and make necessary administrative decisions. In addition to this, the board members are often asked to help specific residents with personal needs. Sometimes it might simply be welcoming a resident into our home for a meal and a visit. The board members

James & Eleri Kerian greet Pierluigi Molla with their two oldest daughters.

are often asked to assist former residents as well. Some help with fundraising duties, including Giving Hearts Day. I've spoken on behalf of the board at pro-life conferences or to high school classes, too."

The board is truly an extension of the Home, bringing its mission and message to other families, neighbors, and communities. Its members help spread the word about the needs existing in our local communities and the importance of cherishing the lives of the unborn and their mothers.

While there is not a high turnover rate with board members, new members are bought on as needed. In 2019 Jessica Knutson and Marissa Kazmierczak joined the board, becoming the youngest and newest board members.

Jessica Knutson has fond memories of the Home from when she was a little girl. As her family dove deeper into their faith, they connected with Father Hils and traveled from Grand Forks, ND, to attend Mass at Saint Stanislaus. Eventually, their family began joining the Home for brunch after Mass, allowing them to encounter the Home and its mission and hospitality.

"One of my earliest memories is going there to stay overnight and help with Geianna and Kassity," Jessica said. "I loved it and couldn't wait to go back and help. I went with my cousin Madeline. We were pretty young, so I'm not sure how much help we were, but it was just about being there and helping with the babies and kids."

Jessica's memories about being involved with the Home as a young girl strike at the importance of presence and, in Jessica's words, simply "being there." This presence is a vital part of living out family life, especially for those who may not have any other family. By extension, those who choose to simply be present in the life of the Home — regardless of age — enter into the work of showing love to each mother and child.

"The Home really is the pro-life movement happening locally," said Jessica. "It's the pro-life movement in action. You think of the pro-life movement as being against abortion, but it's so much more than that, especially for mothers. Being pro-life is supporting the mothers. That was something that was really helpful for me to learn early on, and I learned it through my family's involvement at Saint Gianna's."

While the mission of the Home has always been to help "one mother, one baby, one family at a time," the philosophy of the Home is to show love and share joy to each person and in so doing, invite them into a lifelong relationship with Christ.

"It really shaped our formation," said Jessica, referencing both her and her two brothers. "It's hard for me to put into words how influential it was to be involved from such a young age. I feel like my vocation

Jessica as a young volunteer holding Dominic.

probably started at the Home. It sparked a desire for motherhood and to be close to mothers and women who are pregnant. It became very clear to me that that's what I wanted to do."

Jessica grew up to become a labor and delivery nurse as well as a wife and mother. A picture of Saint Gianna hangs in their kitchen and Jessica asks her intercession frequently.

"Saint Gianna is such a role model to our family," said Jessica. "She's a big part of our life."

After praying for a way to become more involved with the Home, Jessica was approached by Mary Pat to become a board member, allowing her to continue responding to the call she feels to actively be involved in the pro-life movement. Her long history and deep care for the work of the Home make her a perfect candidate to help and serve the Home in this way.

Jessica's story bears witness to God's plan at work in the lives of young people. As children are fed

Craig & Jessica Knutson with their children.

with the truth of God's goodness and the dignity of life, they go on to live beautiful lives filled with peace and great joy.

Marissa Kazmierczak, also a young wife and mother, joined the board around the same time as Jessica.

"I am married to Jon Kazmierczak," said Marissa. "I converted to Catholicism after meeting him and going to church with him. He and his brothers did a lot of work for the Home, and so it was through them that I learned of Saint Gianna's Maternity Home. I had no idea we had something like this in North Dakota let alone in the small town of Warsaw," said Marissa. "The entire work of the Maternity Home is amazing and such a resource. It's super important, especially in our culture today. The world is chaotic, and there are so many people who are pro-choice that don't know about the choices available. They don't know the options. I've had conversations with people at work who are very pro-choice, and they are uneducated. The education provided through the Maternity Home is phenomenal and to have the Home as a choice to share with others is so necessary."

Marissa, who works as a nurse in Grand Forks, has also been inspired by the story of Saint Gianna, especially as she joined the Catholic Church, as a remarkable example of a woman called to live in the world and love others with the radical love of Christ.

"Anxiety about being alone is a big fear for women," said Marissa. "The Maternity Home doesn't just help you through pregnancy until the baby is born. There is so much support through pregnancy and beyond. It lives up to its mission — its focus on one mother, one child, and one family. It's caring for the person as a whole, even after pregnancy."

Marissa may have only learned of Saint Gianna's in recent years but her understanding of the need for this particular mission is what fuels her desire to be on the board, a position which she calls "an honor."

"It's awesome that we have those resources for women who are struggling or don't really know what they want to do while pregnant and they're scared and they actually have somewhere to go to," said Marissa.

Jessica and Marissa were welcomed to the board by members Dolores Grabanski, Joan Schanilec, Colleen Samson, Eleri Kerian, and Robbyne Sands who have been involved from the beginning or very shortly after opening.

"My son Bryan was on the original board," said Dolores. "He passed away unexpectedly in 2005. About a year or two later Mary Pat called and said, 'Would you consider taking Bryan's place on the board?' I said I didn't know. But then I thought about it and called her back. I said yes; I think Bryan would like that. I've been there ever since."

Bryan's involvement with the Home started before the board, with eleven months of Saturdays spent demolishing and renovating the convent before it was usable. A devout Catholic, he would attend Mass as often as possible in addition to Sundays and never backed down from the opportunity to share about the beauty and need to cherish life.

Although Bryan passed at the young age of 43, his holy example has been shown abundantly as people recall his words regarding the opening Saint Gianna's: "If we save just one baby, all of the work will be worth it." This phrase, remembered by various people even now, illuminates the truth of the Home's efforts to safeguard, cherish, and celebrate life.

"Being on the board has drastically changed my life," said Dolores. "Taking the position of board member has been one of the best decisions that I've made. Mary Pat and Father Joseph have given us so much support during the most difficult time of our life. The board members and staff have been treasured friends. I truly feel blessed to be a part of the Home as a board member. It's important to have the Home here because it represents life and it raises awareness to expectant women that they have a safe place to go."

Another board member, Todd Burianek, was a parishioner at Saint Luke's in Veseleyville, ND, when Father Hils arrived.

"I heard about the plans for Saint Gianna's Maternity Home and recall thinking, 'That will never work,'" said Todd. "I am so happy I was wrong."

After the Home was up and running, Mary Pat and Father Hils invited Todd to become a member of the Board of Directors. After a few years of serving on this board, Todd became a member of the Advisory Board, which he still serves to this day.

"Saint Gianna's Maternity Home has been the most important entity I've ever been a part of, notwithstanding my minimal role in it," said Todd. "I've been involved in City Government, the School Board, and other entities, but the Home is the only one that has saved babies' lives. That's far more important than anything else I've ever done."

Over the years, the board members have shared their words on this work in different ways. Here is a collection of their thoughts from the ten-year anniversary of Saint Gianna's:

"In Matthew 19:14, Jesus spoke these words to his disciples when the children were brought to him: 'Let the children come to me, and do not hinder them; for to such belongs the Kingdom of Heaven.' Saint Gianna's Maternity Home in Warsaw reaches out not only to the children but also to their mothers and other family members with a servant's heart filled with love. The endless ways Father Joseph, Mary Pat, the housemothers, and staff members sacrificially share their time, talents, and treasures are too numerous to count and are truly beautiful! These virtuous people pray daily for the grace to cooperate with the Holy Spirit in ministering to each person God places in their path hence providing numerous opportunities for growth in education, holiness, and goodness. Every woman and child is treated with respect and dignity remembering that they are made in the image and likeness of God.

Saint Gianna's Maternity Home, a pro-life home of formation, is truly a safe haven, an apostolate tucked away in a little village where the Holy Spirit, in His gentle and loving way and in His still, small voice speaks to those who are weary from the journey of life. Many pregnant women come to the Home for an opportunity to begin again, resolve issues, see with new eyes, and move forward with a new plan; 'a plan for good and not for evil, a plan with a future and a hope. (Jeremiah 29:11).'

Our holy Patroness, Saint Gianna Beretta Molla, is a beautiful example of a role model that graces the Home. Her sacrificial life is truly one to emulate and promote with the young ladies the Lord brings to us. Her intercession is invaluable in this work that requires much sacrifice and dedication from staff members, to clients, to volunteers. We are so blessed to have a maternity home, a home of prayer, love, and redemption in the state of North Dakota and in our lives." — *Colleen Samson*

"My journey with the Home holds many memories for me. My memories began with my attending school at Saint Anthony's School in Warsaw at the convent, to receive my First Holy Communion.

"The Board of Directors was formed in 2004 for Saint Gianna's Maternity Home. My son, Bryan, was a member of that board. Bryan passed away in 2005. In 2008, I was asked if I would be interested in taking Bryan's place on the board. I think God knew I needed Saint Gianna's Maternity Home in my life at that difficult time. During the renovation, Bryan said, 'If we can save just one baby, it will all be worth it.' It has been worth it. Saint Gianna's has saved the lives of many precious babies! Being a board member at the Home has made my prayer life stronger and has given me the opportunity to do the pro-life work at the Home helping young mothers and their babies." — Dolores Grabanski

"Saint Gianna's Maternity Home has been a blessing to our family in so many ways. Our involvement with Saint Gianna's coincided with my returning to the Catholic faith and my husband joining the Church. During the early years of the Home, Father Hils and Mary Pat played such an important part in establishing a firm foundation to build our faith. Since that time we have been fortunate to serve in many different supporting roles with the Home ranging from board member to babysitter, all equally enjoyable. Regardless of the varied ways we have served, the work carried out at the Home has been a continual reminder to our family that the love of our Lord is still present and fruitful.

"Over the past 10 years, the work of all those involved has been a source of inspiration and hope. The Saint Gianna's Maternity Home has deepened our faith life by keeping our family close to the works of mercy through the daily witness of those fulfilling the duties in serving the women and children residing at the Home. We also see 'faith in action' through the many individuals within the community supporting Saint Gianna's through prayer and financial and material donations. How grateful we are to have been and continue to be a part of building a culture of life! Saint Gianna, pray for us."
— *Jackie Shaft*

"I often think of Saint Gianna's Maternity Home as the pro-life shrine of the prairie. Not because we have tour buses of pilgrims knocking on our doors or because the Home itself is always pristine, peaceful, and serene. No, it is quite the opposite. Most days, I drive by the Home and see bikes and toys on the front steps. When I drop in with a box of donations from the many groups that support our work, I hear noisy toddler footsteps, a crying baby, and laughing mothers in the kitchen. This is the work of the Home — to provide all-encompassing care, formation, and development to the women in our community who need it most. The staff at Saint Gianna's goes beyond diapers and prenatal appointments and facilitates the change our clients need to ensure the best possible start to the next chapter of their lives, whether they parent or place for adoption.

"Each mother I have encountered during my time as a volunteer and as a board member has been a supreme gift to me. The trials they have gone through and the obstacles many of them face humble me. Our ladies are women of dignity and made in His perfect image and the children they carry are unique, unrepeatable, precious human beings. Saint Gianna's is a missionary to all who come seeking aid. When most people think of a shrine, they think of something physically created to give glory to God. While our Home and chapel are certainly beautiful, it is our work together with our residents, supported by our generous benefactors that really gives Him the greatest glory. My family is proud to support this wonderful gem in the most pro-life, and we are thankful to those who join us in supporting Saint Gianna's." — *Eleri Kerian*

"In the darkness of the world Christ is our light. The young pregnant women that come to Saint Gianna's Maternity Home feel that light and the warmth of Christ the second they arrive; this is the light that can dispel the darkness and rid them of their fear. The Maternity Home is that beacon of light shining itself in the darkness and shining itself into the souls of the women that live there and to the entire community. The staff and director, Mary Pat Jahner, truly do carry the light of Christ to all they meet. They work tirelessly, planting the seeds of faith in these young women, and then cultivating and nurturing the seeds by their constant example of virtue. The fruits of their work are revealed in the births of 94 babies that have been born and in the numerous conversions that have taken place within the hearts of the mothers. That same light has even been carried to me while I was pregnant with my 6th and 7th babies as they brought me many meals and prayed countless prayers for me.

"By the grace of God, the cooperation of those that work there, and the prayerful support of so many, the light of Christ is shining and lighting up the world through Saint Gianna's Maternity Home! Through the intercession of Saint Gianna, we ask God to continue His blessing upon the Maternity Home for many more decades to come." — *Robbyne Sands*

"Faith in action — these three simple words define what I have seen and experienced over the years that I have been involved with Saint Gianna's Maternity Home. Prior to becoming a part of the apostolate, my sole pro-life activity was to write an occasional check to a local pregnancy help center. But God wanted more from me!

"It has been an eye-opening and faith-building experience to be a part of this pro-life movement up close and real through the work of the Maternity Home. We witness lives changed, hope given, and mothers choosing life for their unborn children. Some women make the difficult yet generous

> "We witness lives changed, hope given, and mothers *choosing life* for their unborn children."

decision to place their babies for adoption while others choose to lovingly parent their child. God is at work here…in every situation, with every tear that is shed, with every difficult choice that is made, and with every prayer that is prayed. I thank and praise God for the privilege of being a part of Saint Gianna's Maternity Home. I have been blessed and have received so much more than I have given." — *Joan Schanilec*

"Serving as Chaplain and Spiritual Director for the Saint Gianna Maternity Home has enriched my own spiritual well-being as daily life at the Home presents rewards, challenges, joys, and strenuous spirit labor. As I work with residents, and even with staff, I am reminded of the tremendous importance of fatherhood, especially spiritual fatherhood, a role I am immersed in while serving here. I can see the absolute need for the father in the family dynamic, and that biological fatherhood also should be coupled with spiritual fatherhood. A father gives life and protects that life; and in a similar way, spiritual fatherhood gives spiritual life and should nurture and protect the spiritual life of those for whom they care.

"As I help these ladies on their journey, it is uplifting to my soul to see them grow spiritually and in their prayer life. I can see them become more and more mindful of the need to turn to God for help, guidance, and strength through prayer as they make their way to recovering healthier lives for themselves and their babies. And at times when they slide backward, this helps me then to grow more in piety as I need to turn to God in prayer, interceding on their behalf. This is what a father, and in my case — a spiritual father – should do: to give and even sacrifice oneself for the benefit of those in their care. This is what Our Lord has done for me as He gave His life for me and for all of us. Jesus tells us in the Gospel: 'I came that they might have life and have it more abundantly' (Jn 10:10), and 'there is no greater love than to lay down one's life for a friend' (Jn 15:13). I pray that I may continue as a spiritual father here at the Saint Gianna Maternity Home to lead these mothers and their children closer to their Father in Heaven." — *Father Joseph Christensen, FMI* [9]

Father Joseph preforms hospital baptism for newborn Kcoyn.

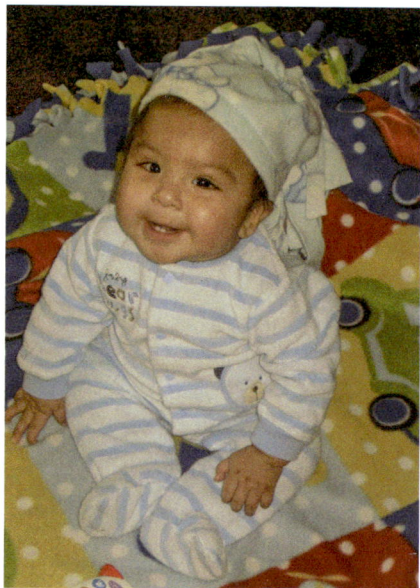

Aiden Joseph

Jemma Jade

Father Joseph explaining Saint Gianna's relics to the Rilie and Ashley Morgan Family.

April 21, 2018 Celebrating Gianna Emanuela's 56th birthday.

Devan with her son Finn, placing a rose in front of Saint Gianna's picture at our opening Mass of the Anniversary year.

Aubrey, with her birthmother, Hannah.

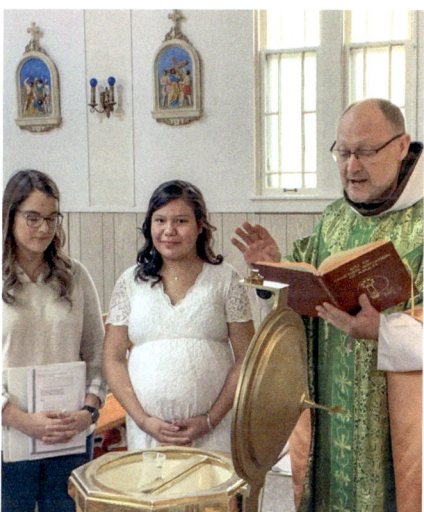

JayAnn's Baptism at her home parish in Fort Totten, ND with housemother Dani, her godmother, and Father Joseph.

Housemothers and moms carving pumpkins.

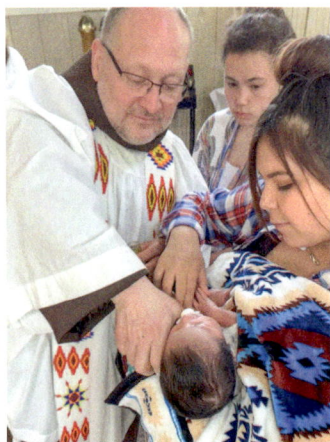

Father Joseph baptizing Jeremiah James, son of KK, at her home parish in Ft. Totten, ND

Bishop Folda receiving Saint Gianna's relic from Michelle Useldinger at our 10 year Anniversary Mass.

Kassity placing the crown on Blessed Mother during May Crowning.

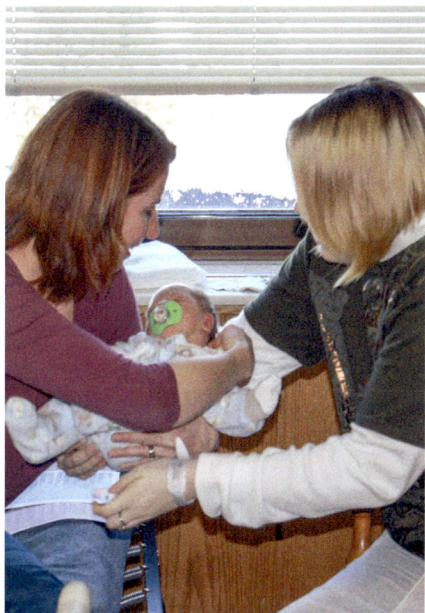

Sam placing newborn Jacob in the arms of his adoptive mother, Jen.

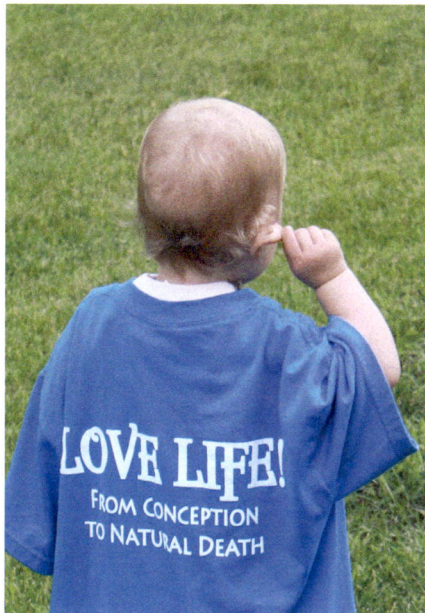

Dominic in his 5K T-Shirt.

Housemother Jess taking a break with Ryland.

Brooklynn playing Peek a Boo in the chapel.

Board members; Darrin Muggli, Colleen Samson, Dolores Grabanski, Joan Schanilec, Director, Mary Pat Jahner, Jackie and Grant Shaft, Robbynne Sands and Todd Burianek.

Gracie, with Carla, her adoptive mom and Crissy, her birthmother.

Dena, with Colette.

Fernando

Mariana, pictured with Teddy and his adoptive parents, Tyler and Rachel.

MaryAnn exercising.

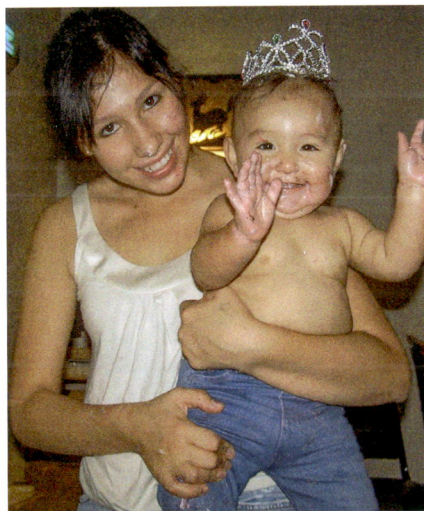

Shanna, with Geianna on her first birthday.

Whitney, with Keegan.

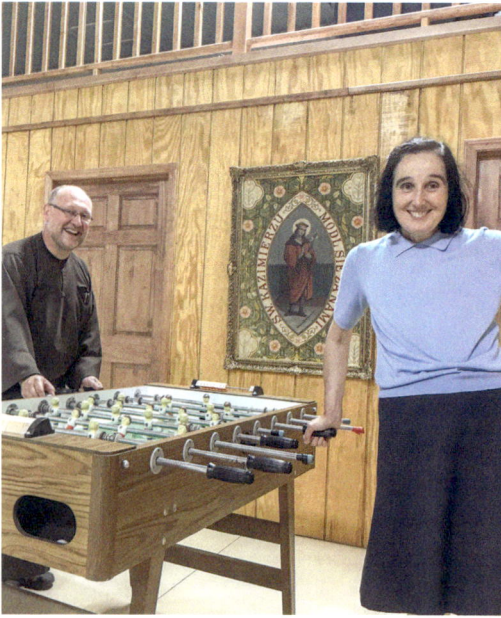

Gianna Emanuela enjoying the victory.

His Eminence Cardinal Raymond Burke, who is an Honorary Advisor to our home, pictured with Father Joseph.

Praying outside of the abortion facility.

Three of our "little ones" ready for the Christmas Eve procession before mass.

Housemothers

Over the years many women have served the Home through the role of a housemother, working full-time for Saint Gianna's and living with the women who reside there. Housemothers fulfill a deeply human need for family and stability, aspects that are necessary to the flourishing of a family. This live-in position includes a task list that is constantly changing. As the needs of the women who live at the Home change, so does the job of the housemother on duty. Just like a family living in one house, everyone — housemother and residents — must learn to grow together.

While the vision for the Maternity Home is to help women who are struggling through crisis pregnancies, the unique role of a housemother invites the women who hold this position to change and grow themselves. For each learning experience of a resident, there is one for a housemother as well, as they open their hearts to each woman who moves into the Home.

Many housemothers, through their experience, have felt prepared for becoming wives and mothers, developed a deeper understanding of their Catholic faith and the pro-life movement, and experienced profound peace in learning to do God's will in their own lives as modeled through Saint Gianna and the work of the Maternity Home.

The following stories are witnesses from only a handful of housemothers who have spent time working at Saint Gianna's Maternity Home over its first twenty years. Like the residents, they have come from different backgrounds and various experiences. Through the grace of God, the housemothers have been called to give of themselves in this unique ministry. By living out the call to faith and service, they are able to share the love of Christ with every person who walks through the doors of the Saint Gianna and Pietro Molla Maternity Home.

The Gift of Witness: Housemother Jessica

Jessica Wasko (now Gabriel) served the Maternity Home tirelessly and with grace and virtue for three years, between 2010 and 2013. Saint Gianna's Home was so blessed by her selfless and generous service. During her last days with us, she wrote a short reflection that she gave at a celebration on August 17, 2013.

Hello, my name is Jessica and I have been blessed to be a part of the work at Saint Gianna's as a housemother for almost three years. My time here is coming to a close and as I prepare to leave, I have been reflecting a lot on my time here and what I will take with me. I thought I would give you a little glimpse into my life as a housemother at Saint Gianna's.

Jessica Gabriel holding one of our newborns.

When I tell people that I am a housemother at a maternity home, it is always followed by the question 'what does that mean?' An easy answer to that question is that I supervise the Home, provide support to the residents, drive our residents to appointments, teach classes, cook, and clean. If I was to get technical, I could also say I am a landscaper, a photographer, an editor, a teacher, a window washer, a cook for up to 50, a master Sam's Club shopper, and the official food critic.

I'm sure my fellow housemothers could add dozens of other guises we have had to take on and while all of these tasks have made it a busy three years, I would not say that those are the things I will necessarily recall. More so, I believe I will remember a truly unique gift in which I was able to witness and experience the things that make Saint Gianna's special.

I witnessed women that walked into our home afraid and alone but set aside their own fears and heroically chose life for their baby. I witnessed the bravery and selfless love of the mothers who chose to share this gift of life and exemplified the true meaning of sacrifice as they placed their newborn into the hands of their adoptive parents. I witnessed the tears of joy and gratitude of adoptive parents as a child is entrusted to their care and years of prayers are finally answered. I witnessed a mother's wonder as she saw the baby within her for the first time at her ultrasound and listened to a perfect beating heart. I witnessed the very first moment of a life. I witnessed a precious baby's first smiles, first laughs, first tooth, and first steps. And I've shared in the joy of mothers as they watch their babies grow.

I witnessed the tears of despair, the pain from a lifetime of hurts, confusion, and anger, but I have also witnessed healing and conversion. And I witnessed that despair, pain, confusion, and anger turn into hope, joy, self-confidence, and trust. I witnessed and was called on by the example of my coworkers as they constantly put themselves aside in order to serve day after day. I have never witnessed them asking for anything in return. I witnessed the kindness and generosity of friends, neighbors, and strangers, whose support has inspired and uplifted us in times of need. This is how I spent the last three years of my life.

Saint Gianna's will always have a special place in my heart. I am truly honored to be a member of this family and I would like to wholeheartedly thank all of you who have contributed to our work. We would be at a loss without the generosity, prayers, and sacrifice of many of you here today.

Wanting Good for Each Other: Housemother Dena

Dena Maciborski (now O'Connor) found her way to Saint Gianna's Maternity Home as one of the first housemothers from 2007 to 2011 after having been involved in pro-life activity from a young age.

"I remember marching in the 4th of July parade wearing pro-life shirts with the Knights of Columbus growing up," reminisced Dena. "In college, I prayed outside abortion facilities and I did the Crossroads Pro-Life walk across the country in 2000. We walked across the country with teams, and we would pray outside abortion clinics, speak at churches and offer up our walking for the unborn. I always had the desire to continue doing pro-life work, but I didn't know what it would look like. One of the questions I remember thinking to myself while praying at abortion clinics was, 'After they choose life, how do we help them? We speak to them and encourage them to choose life for their baby, but how do you follow up with that? What do you offer them after they make that decision? What can I do?' That was my interior thought."

Dena discovered the housemother position at Saint Gianna's Maternity Home while she was looking for a different work direction in life. The Home sounded like a promising opportunity to concretely live out the pro-life mission, answering the questions she had previously asked herself.

"The Maternity Home gives women an option," said Dena. "It gives them hope, and it's an actual choice. It's a hopeful choice. It's a future. It's not an ending but a beginning. In our culture, the so-called 'choice' is destructive — it leaves women with years of agony for their so-called choice of abortion. With the Home, whether they decide to parent or place for adoption, there is still hope. There is still a future. It shows them another way, and it's truly a culture of life."

Dena's words capture the heart of the housemother's job at the Maternity Home as one who ministers to women who need support after choosing life.

"I think back to the occasions where I was speaking with women or men outside of abortion clinics, trying to persuade them to choose life and not knowing what experience in life they are coming from," said Dena. "We need to be able to offer help beyond just that instance of encounter. There is further assistance, and it's not just choosing life for your baby. There's an actual place for them, the mothers, and a way to help them through their pregnancy and beyond."

Housemothers at the Maternity Home step into the lives of women when they are afraid, uncertain, and stressed. For Dena, one of the biggest takeaways from her experience as a housemother related to the way she got to know each woman personally.

"To not judge people before you experience people personally is so important," said Dena. "Everybody has a story, and I think getting to know people one-on-one is way different than assuming you know who they are. Knowing as many different women and children who came through the Home during my four years there, you learn that there are different ways to relate to people and connect. Learning to connect with someone and try to understand where they are coming from is so necessary — both in pro-life work and in our daily lives."

For a housemother, the task of getting to know and connect with the women is not a one-way street. The role of a housemother includes both giving and receiving love.

"As much as you want to see them happy, they also want to see you happy," said Dena. "It's like living in that familial atmosphere where you all want the good for each other. Granted that there were tough days, but for the most part, it was just enjoying life together, living everyday life with these women. It's not out of the ordinary – it is just everyday life with every person that comes through the door and you get to know them personally. As much as you want to help them, they are also helping you. It's a give and take."

To this day, Dena remains in contact with some of the women she worked with during her time at the Home. She is a godmother to a baby boy that was born while she was there, and the relationships she created are more akin to family. The Saint Gianna and Pietro Molla Maternity Home intentionally chose to operate with housemothers, honoring the truth that family life is hard but beautiful.

In this way, the women who come to the Home are invited both to receive and share. Each woman who arrives has gifts and strengths as well as needs and weaknesses. In the context of a family, the women can start viewing themselves with greater self-respect and recognize the areas where growth is needed.

"The women would learn their different gifts and talents," said Dena as she reflected on this experience. "Like Sam — she made knoephla, and I had no idea that she could cook, and it was so good. There are things we don't necessarily volunteer about ourselves, but when you live with others, you get to know them. Tara could play the piano and I loved listening to her play. We'd be in the basement and listen to her playing upstairs; it was so great."

Dena's time at the Home was a source of blessings and growth. She poured herself out by loving the women and encountering the joy and peace that comes by offering oneself to God through sacrificial love in service to others.

Common Ground: Housemother Lori

Lori Seiwert (now Boyne) found Saint Gianna's Maternity Home while searching for jobs during her senior year of college. Lori had never been to North Dakota, but trusted in God's providence leading her to the Home.

"When family members and friends would ask where I was working, they always gave me a puzzled look when I told them I worked and lived at a maternity home," said Lori Boyne, who started as a housemother in 2012. "I would always explain it like this: I just

Matt & Lori Boyne with their children.

live life alongside the residents. We eat together, pray together, and learn together. Usually, their past lives were anything but normal, so our job was to give them stability and normalcy in a very uncertain time in their lives."

The work as a housemother was "very much outside of [her] comfort zone," yet appeared to Lori as an opportunity to live out the values of the pro-life movement.

"Actions speak louder than words," Lori said. "The Maternity Home isn't just marching in DC and praying at abortion clinics, though these are also very important. The Maternity Home is taking the next step and actually acting on what the pro-life movement claims to believe."

> "The Maternity Home is *taking the next step* and actually acting on what the pro-life movement claims to believe."

Every life from conception until natural death, is worthy, unrepeatable, and irreplaceable. This includes not only the precious babies in the womb, the sleepy newborns, and the bumbling toddlers, but also the mothers of these children who may come from broken backgrounds and difficult situations. The pro-life movement is as much about a deep respect and support for the women who find themselves pregnant and with nowhere to go as it is for protecting the innocent lives they bring into the world.

"As a mother now, I constantly remind myself that the small tasks are done throughout the day — cooking, praying, playing games, and the like — create some of the most important moments," said Lori. "The Home isn't changing thousands of lives at a time but the ripple effect is endless. I make sure that the little things are what I focus on with my own little family now."

By recognizing the great importance of small moments each day as opportunities for growth in holiness and love, the housemothers help residents experience and understand the importance of family life.

"I always loved that everyone who lived at Saint Gianna's had a different story to tell," said Lori. "Living in the same house gave you common ground. You were there for a reason. Diversity creates bonds as you grow together. I hope the residents learned just as much from me as I learned from them during my time there."

The common ground of the Maternity Home helped prepare Lori for her vocation as a wife and mother.

"Since leaving the Home, I have become a mother myself," said Lori. "It is life-changing in a way that I didn't understand when I worked at the Maternity Home. I am grateful that the mothers there not only choose life but also humbled themselves in such a way as to reach out for help and allow others into their lives, to entrust their little ones into our care."

It is this spirit of respect and understanding that invites the women who move into the Maternity Home to experience the love of Christ, often amidst uncertainty and loneliness.

Each year at the Christmas party, the Maternity Home family participates in a tradition from Saint Faustina's Convent – the tradition of being chosen by a saint for the year. Lori recalls her last Christmas party as a housemother and receiving a gift that she would hold close to her heart as she left the Home to get married.

"At my last Christmas party there, instead of having a saint for the year, Mary Pat picked out virtues of Saint Gianna for us to choose for the year," said Lori. "Others drew joy and courage but the virtue I drew was long-suffering. I was almost angry that God chose me to have that virtue because I knew it wasn't a mistake. That was the year I was going to get married and start the next chapter of my life, but I didn't want it to start out on a sour note. What I didn't know at the time was that Long Suffering was the virtue I was going to take with me into the next chapter and beyond. It's not a curse or a bad omen, but a virtue that reminds us that our Catholic faith involves suffering — holy suffering, suffering for the sake of ourselves and the sake of those around us. Since leaving the Home, I have experienced physical suffering and emotional suffering both in myself and in those I love but, because of that foreshadowing, I know those moments are not supposed to lead me farther away from God, but that I should cling to Him all the more. It's the ongoing gift Saint Gianna has given me for the rest of my life."

Spirit of Hospitality: Housemother Jessica

Similar to other housemothers, Jessica Gabriel recalls feeling led by God to work at Saint Gianna and Pietro Molla Maternity Home and recalls her time spent as a housemother as one filled with many graces.

"I was in my senior year of college when I applied for Saint Gianna's," said Jessica. "I knew that I wanted to do some sort of service-type work, but I wasn't sure what I wanted to do. My friend told me about the mission and her own experiences with Saint Gianna's. After talking to her, I knew that I wanted to work at a maternity home, and I applied to more than one. I even went to visit more than one, but when I went to interview at Saint Gianna's, I fell in love with it."

Something that set the Saint Gianna and Pietro Molla Maternity Home apart is the way the housemothers truly integrate into the lives of the women living at the Home, forming a family. While many might think of Saint Gianna's as a temporary shelter for women, those who are involved reveal that the mission of the Home is the formation of a family. The familial bonds formed during that time are not broken or left behind when women leave the Home.

"Saint Gianna's is more family-style living," said Jessica. "The Catholic nature of it is incorporated into the whole day. I think of being a housemother as living with the women, creating a family environment to provide them support during their pregnancies. When I think back on the job, a lot of it was just living a family life: cooking meals together, going to doctor appointments, going on summer vacation."

Similar to family life, it is not just one person who is transformed by the experience but the whole family that grows and changes together. The women who live at the Home uproot their lives, make drastic changes, and open themselves up to a new way of living. The women who choose to serve as housemothers do this as well by opening up their lives to create a respectful, loving, welcoming environment for the residents.

"Something that I think I grew in during this time was the spirit of hospitality and a love for it," said Jess. "It is such a welcoming place, and there are so many people involved. Any time we got a new resident or someone was coming to dinner it was always a big to do. We were going to create a great experience for them, and I think that's something that I'll keep with me."

"The spirit of hospitality modeled by Saint Gianna herself includes providing physical comforts like good meals and *openness of heart* to those being served."

The spirit of hospitality modeled by Saint Gianna herself includes providing physical comforts like good meals and openness of heart to those being served. It requires humbling oneself, like Christ did through the Incarnation, and it is this spirit that the staff of Saint Gianna's strives to emulate.

Praying For Them Out of Love: Housemother Ashley

Ashley Bezdicek (now Morgan) was a housemother for about a year and a half, beginning in 2008, and carries the lessons from her time at Saint Gianna's in her daily life as a wife and mother. Ashley learned of Saint Gianna and Pietro's through her roommate and felt the Holy Spirit leading her to be involved in the work of the Home.

Ashley holding one of our new little ones.

"It was the fall of 2008 and I was student teaching," said Ashley. "I didn't have plans for after graduation, but I didn't feel ready to jump into a full-time Art teaching position yet. I happened to be living with Hayley (Schanilec) Kaffar at the time. Her mom Joan came to visit and was telling us all about Saint Gianna's Maternity Home. My heart was drawn to it as she was talking about it. Another roommate of mine was very active in the pro-life movement on campus, but I never felt called to join her, although I felt very pro-life and would pray at the abortion clinic with her. I remember thinking that the Home was a very real and personal way to promote life. Joan said I should see if there was a housemother opening. I contacted Mary Pat Jahner, the director, but she said there were no openings at the time. I decided to make a trip to tour the Home anyway since it tugged at my heart so much. I ended up applying for a youth ministry job at Saint Francis de Sales Church in Moorhead, MN. I was offered the job, but after a week of discerning, it just didn't feel right. I turned down the job without any other job in sight. That weekend I attended the Marian Eucharistic Congress and ran into Mary Pat. She told me that one of the current housemothers needed to leave unexpectedly and there was now an opening. I don't recall all the details after that, but God paved the way and made it clear where I was supposed to be."

While Ashley had planned to become an art teacher, God led her on a path to use her education and talents in another way.

"Prayer was a regular part of life there," said Ashley. "I loved living in a place with a chapel. As a housemother, my role was to clean, cook, mentor, and help the residents. I personally set up and did art with the residents using my art education background and passion for creating beauty. I think it was fun for them. It was a joy getting to know each and every one of the residents that came and went."

Each housemother, staff member, and volunteer brings their personal gifts and talents to the life of the Home, reflecting one's call to generously share with others what one has been given.

Living together presents difficulties that offer opportunities for increased trust in God. The goal at Saint Gianna's is not the work of perfecting personalities but the pursuit of peace and joy in Christ, who shows us that love and family life require prayer, generosity, and sacrifice.

"Working at Saint Gianna's was a place of learning for me, especially learning to pray for people even when they don't always change the way we want them to or think they should," said Ashley. "You pray for them out of love and ask mercy on them, even if you don't see the prayers answered. You entrust them to God's care and God's timing and then leave it to Him."

Ashley's testimony highlights how the staff's role is not to take control of the residents' lives but provide a place for the women to open their hearts to God's love and mercy. The Home stands in deep surrender to the providence and will of God, respecting the dignity and free will of all.

This ordering towards God and His plan for us stayed with Ashley as she became a wife and mother years later.

"I will never forget Mary Pat's number one instruction," said Ashley. "It has been very helpful in my life now as a mother of four of my own children. Peace is the result of order. It was something I had to grow in. The importance of it at the Home was vital because some of the situations the women came from were disordered or difficult. The order of the Home could be a safe haven for them, rest from the stress of the world and their situations."

While Ashley went to Saint Gianna's to give, she left taking these lessons with her into her next stage of life, in which the Home played a crucial role.

"Working at the Maternity Home led to my vocation of marrying Rilie Morgan," said Ashley. "This was something only God could plan. Mary Pat and the Maternity Home were always supportive of me as that relationship blossomed, grew and we got married. I am so grateful."

Rilie's mother, Linda Babinski, was involved with the Home through her job and introduced Ashley to Rilie. Their wedding took place across the street at Saint Stanislaus Catholic Church, with a great presence of those involved at the Saint Gianna and Pietro Molla Maternity Home . Ashley and Rilie included many of the children who were at the Home during their relationship, some taking the role of ring bearer or flower girl. Ashley and Rilie recognized that their relationship was blessed by the example and spirit of Saint Gianna and the Home.

"Living and working at the Maternity Home was rewarding," said Ashley. "I will always cherish my time there. I will never forget each of the women I served and their little ones. I made wonderful friendships and continue to look up to Mary Pat as a wonderful woman of God and friend. One of the biggest lessons was that life is beautiful and it's very important to celebrate it."

> "One of the biggest lessons was that *life is beautiful* and it's very important to celebrate it."

Showing Women Their Worth: Housemother Madelyn

Madelyn Larson (now Long) learned of Saint Gianna's as a young girl through her family, whose history has been influenced greatly by both Saint Gianna and the Maternity Home.

"I first learned of the Home when my aunt Natalie Wavra introduced us when I was around 10 years old," said Madelyn. "We started getting involved around Christmas. We would get a Christmas list from Mary Pat for the mothers and families at the Home. My aunts, grandma and girl cousins always made an event out of it: we would shop all day, sometimes two days, then have a sleepover and the next day do the wrapping. Sometimes we would make Christmas cookies, too.

We always looked forward to that time of year.

Madelyn fondly remembers this tradition which first sparked her interest in the Home.

"I always dreamed of being a housemother there," said Madelyn. "I was, and still am, in awe of new life. When I approached the summer between freshman and sophomore year of college I asked Mary Pat if I could volunteer for the summer while I was home (East Grand Forks, MN). She received me so joyfully. Through God's grace, I ended up staying for another year as a housemother."

Madelyn & Michael Long with their children.

Madelyn reflects that she received many graces in the time that she spent in service at the Home.

"Now being a mother myself, I look back at my role as a housemother and see some similarities that prepared me well for this vocation, and for this, I am so grateful," said Madelyn.

The vibrancy and joy of the family is at the heart of the seemingly mundane tasks of a housemother.

"Being a housemother had physical, emotional, and spiritual aspects to it," said Madelyn. "We took care of a lot of practical things such as cleaning, cooking, running errands, going to doctors' appointments, helping with a bath, holding or watching a little one to give mom a break, and more. Emotionally, there is a lot of listening. Listening to the mothers vent, share their stories, and voice their worries or frustrations without judgment. We were there to encourage the mothers and celebrate and walk with them on their journey, instilling a sense of hope in them. Spiritually, as a housemother, it is showing the women their worth. Not by speaking it directly but in the way we treat them and showing that they are worth fighting for because Jesus shed His blood for all of us. Spiritually we try to show them that life matters, including their worries, fears, joys, even their past, present, and future."

The deep need each person has for God's love is especially visible in the women who come from broken homes or abusive situations. The schedule and structure of the Home fosters an environment where the women can be ministered to physically, emotionally, and spiritually. The housemother position is vital to carrying out this ministry.

"In a culture that says life is disposable, Saint Gianna's Maternity Home says that life is irreplaceable and that every life matters," said Madelyn. "Every life is priceless. I think this message is so important to counteract the toxic, consumerist mindset of the world today. It is so easy to get into the mindset of just throwing things away; it creeps into all aspects of life and has now flowed over into how people treat each other."

By spending time regularly in Christ's presence each day in prayer, the staff of the Home stays spiritually rooted. Housemothers invite the residents to view their lives along with the lives of their children as irreplaceable and abundantly cherished by God.

"Mass and Holy Hours were offered daily in the Home," said Madelyn. "As a housemother, this time to spend with Jesus was so crucial and sustaining. To pray for the mothers, to ask for the grace to serve the mothers and their families with love, to just be in the Lord's presence and praise Him."

The spiritual life of the Home truly is the foundation of the household, which is also reflected physically as the Visitation Chapel in the center of the building.

"God showed up time and again," said Madelyn. "When we were out of diapers, a random box would show up on the doorstep in the exact size we needed. God is so generous and cannot be outdone. He always provides. While working at Saint Gianna's, I learned that in order to live life, you have to give. And if you give of yourself with love, there is always joy and grace to accompany it."

> "
> "I learned that in order to live life, you have to give. And if you give of yourself with love, there is always *joy* and *grace* to accompany it."

It's About Relationships: Housemother Tegan

Housemother Tegan Chesney (now Burkhardt) learned of Saint Gianna's Maternity Home through the University of Notre Dame's Summer Service Learning Program (SSLP). The children of board members Grant and Jackie Shaft attended Notre Dame, and when the Shafts learned of the summer program, they thought Saint Gianna's Maternity Home would be a great addition to the summer volunteer options through the university.

"The Center for Social Concerns at the University of Notre Dame partners with nonprofits throughout the country to provide meaningful summer positions to students through the Summer Service Learning Program," said Tegan. "I was interested in doing something like this the summer after my sophomore year when I was nineteen years old. I have always adored children and the goodness that they bring, so I knew I wanted to participate in something involving babies and children. When I learned about the mission of the Maternity Home and heard that I would be part of the first participating group of students from Notre Dame, I was excited by the prospect of being part of something so meaningful."

"I have a tendency to throw myself into things without thinking them through," said Tegan with a laugh. "I had a loose idea of what a maternity home was, but I was surprised by how much of a home it was. I pictured more of an institution than a home. I talked with Mary Pat on the phone before, and she sent me a few books, but it wasn't until I arrived that I truly understood.

Tegan described her role as a housemother: "A housemother wears many different hats, and I think that is part of the wonder of the Maternity Home — housemothers do whatever is needed and whatever is desired to help bring peace and love to the Home," said Tegan.

Tegan believes the work of the Home bridges the gap between those with gifts to offer and those in need. She describes, in reflecting, on her summer at the Maternity Home and the ways it influenced her understanding of Catholic ministry.

"The Maternity Home is trying to break down barriers," said Tegan. "It's about relationships. We are here doing our best to lift each other up and provide support and stability for residents when they might not have it otherwise. It's about finding ways to bring people's gifts and natural relationships to make a community."

"I think it was a very formative time for me," said Tegan. "It was definitely a learning experience. I think the biggest thing I noticed was the large amounts of love and generosity there. It was a very humbling experience — I reflect a lot on the experience and what I've learned from it. The mothers were witnesses of great courage and trust. Although their futures were unknown, the mothers understood that the life inside them was worth any cost on their part."

A Place To Be Brave: Assistant Director Morgan

Morgan Christensen learned of Saint Gianna's Maternity Home through her uncle, Father Joseph Christensen FMI. She first came to Warsaw in the summer of 2013 after graduating from high school. During this summer she helped with the JMI summer camps hosted by her uncle's religious order.

"During those two weeks I got a little glimpse into the work of Saint Gianna's," said Morgan. "I learned quite a bit about the inspiring Saint and got to see how they've incorporated her heroic example of motherhood into the daily workings of the

Morgan with Brooklynn

Home and its mission of one baby, one mother, one family at a time. I returned each summer after and stayed a little longer each time. Then, in January of 2016, I moved out to North Dakota to work at Saint Gianna's."

Since she started working at the Home in 2016, Morgan has learned well the "job description" of the housemother.

"The question of 'what does a housemother do' is typically met with a bit of a smile or a laugh," said Morgan. "This reaction is simply because it is both an easy and hard question to answer. The easy answer is that you are as much as the title states. You are the motherly role model, the example the residents look to and go to for guidance on everything life is throwing at them. But, as a housemother, you wear many hats from day to day, and that is the difficult part to answer. No two days have been the same in nearly all the years I have worked at Saint Gianna's. One day you could be a cook, a gardener, or a tutor and the next day you are an editor and a firefighter. So, in short, you do a lot of things a typical mother does to keep order and structure in a home. You take residents to appointments, make meals, make sure grades are satisfactory, and make sure the day-to-day life goes smoothly."

In reflecting on her many years spent working at Saint Gianna's, Morgan recognizes that the learning process between residents and housemothers goes both ways. "When it comes to the women we work with, I think I have learned as much from them as I hope they have learned from me," said Morgan. "I have learned to have deeper gratitude for my own family, especially my parents, and to be more patient, kind, and compassionate. I've learned you can't judge someone's story by the chapter you walked in on. I have become more aware of how my words and actions influence those around me. But it is not just the women we strive to help that I have learned from. It is also those I work alongside, from the board to the Director and the housemothers. Every single person I have worked with has brought their own gifts to Saint Gianna's. And by their examples, I have grown so much since I began here. I have grown in humility and faith, and I have stepped out of my comfort zones."

Morgan's deepening gratitude for her family, especially her parents, comes from seeing the experience of so many women who do not have support from their family or parents. When broken homes become normalized, women who experience an unexpected pregnancy do not have the resources and support available to help them bring life into the world. It is here that the work of Saint Gianna's Maternity Home unfolds, drawing women into a loving family structure that can provide them the opportunity to experience love and grow.

"The focus on family and community living at Saint Gianna's is so integral to its success," said Morgan. "It provides an environment that gives the residents an abundance of love, support, and stability that many have not experienced before. It gives them a good example and foundation to build off when they are ready to move on from Saint Gianna's with their little ones. No two women's stories are the same, but living as a family gives them people to lean on and relate to. It gives them a support system they can count on to help them in good times and in bad."

> "No two women's stories are the same, but living as a family gives them people to lean on and relate to. It gives them a *support system* they can count on to help them in good times and in bad."

Even after women leave the Home with their children, Mary Pat and the Home remain a source of support for them. The volunteers and donors of Saint Gianna's help these women when they need it, which includes taking them into their homes, offering rides, helping with job applications and housing, and many other needs.

"The mission of Saint Gianna's is quite simple yet so important in today's society," said Morgan. "I believe that its message of life is so vital because fear is so prevalent and is used so often as a tool to dismantle God's message to us. As Pope Saint John Paul II said, 'The human being is single, unique, and unrepeatable, someone thought of and chosen from eternity, someone called and identified by name.' Society uses fear to try and silence the truth. This is especially true in the lives of each woman who walks through our doors. They come to us from all walks of life, and they are so often afraid — afraid of judgment and ridicule, from those they love, or afraid of those who have never bothered to ask their story. They come here to find a place to be brave and learn God's truth about them and their precious, unrepeatable little ones."

Residents

Saint Gianna's Maternity Home would not exist without the mothers who make the courageous decision to start a better life for themselves and their children by calling this place "home". Their stories could fill a volume of their own.

The residents of the Maternity Home choose life, not just for their babies, but also for themselves. As these women become mothers, they experience the hope and promise brought by a new life. Regardless of the situation that leads a woman to Saint Gianna's doorstep, the message of Christ's love is waiting to greet them.

A Saint For A Mother: Emily & Enya's Story

Emily was seventeen when she came to Saint Gianna's. She had grown up in a Catholic family and shared about what brought her to the Home.

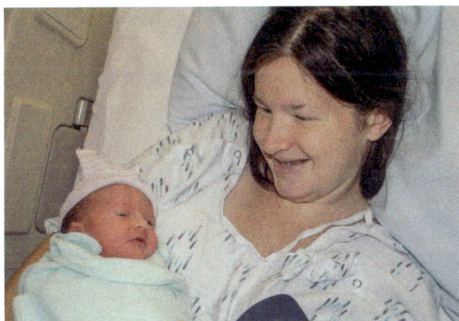

Emily holding her newborn daughter, Enya.

"My parents weren't thrilled I was pregnant," Emily said. "They didn't want me to keep the baby. They didn't want abortion at all, but they wanted me to seriously consider adoption. I ended up needing some mental health treatment while I was pregnant, and we made the decision as a team that I would go to Saint Gianna's for the rest of my pregnancy. It was a tough spot for my parents to be in — they weren't excited I was going to Saint Gianna's, but they understood it was a good option."

Emily recounted moving to the Home from Georgia: "We arrived in the middle of a storm," said Emily. "I thought I had seen storms when I lived in Nebraska, but I had not seen a storm like we did that night. We were driving on the highway, and my Mom said to watch out for tornadoes. That was my welcome to North Dakota. But I thought the property was beautiful — the setting was so quiet."

Emily could not have anticipated how her time at the Home would change her life. The decision to move to Warsaw was a turning point in her pregnancy that involved great sacrifice. Emily had to uproot her life, move somewhere foreign, and surrender certain freedoms.

"Up until I moved to Saint Gianna's my pregnancy was so negative," said Emily. "I had never lived away from my parents, and Mary Pat was the first person who really said anything positive about my pregnancy. It was nice to be in an environment where I didn't have to worry about how I felt or how I looked and be able to talk to other young women who were in a similar situation.

"My best memories are from the Guardian Angel room," recalled Emily. "We used to sneak off there if we wanted to hide from the housemothers. We'd go in there for a few minutes and pretend one was breastfeeding and needing a break. I'm sure they knew what we were doing. I also remember when my water broke. It broke during church, of course, and Mary Pat said, 'We have time, we should have lunch before we go to the hospital.'"

Emily laughed while recalling these memories, before continuing, "The housemother Becky had made rolls and German chocolate cake the day before, so my lunch consisted of ramen noodles, German chocolate cake, and rolls. Mary Pat told me I'd have to tell them over and over what my last meal was, but I just said, 'Well, this is what we're doing.'"

Emily's stay at the Maternity Home was relatively short—around five months total—yet this time changed her life. She recognizes that this time profoundly impacted the direction of her life, and attributes this to the people she met there.

"Mary Pat is probably the least judgmental person I have ever met in my life, and this was a huge change for me. I never felt like she was judgmental or condescending about the pregnancy or the situation I was in. She wanted me to move forward and work with what I had. She wanted to get me what I needed to be successful, and that was really, really different for me. She's a planner, but she was very good if something unexpected hit; it was like she was planning for that, too."

Emily was raised Catholic and had received all the sacraments before arriving at the Home, but she wasn't familiar with Saint Gianna's story at all when she moved to Warsaw.

"I didn't think saints were normal before I was at the Home," said Emily. "You always read those stories where they did super duper things or were perfect, and I thought, 'Well, that's unattainable.' But learning Saint Gianna's story gave me hope. It's basically there's a saint because she's a mom which I think is pretty cool. I don't think moms get quite enough recognition, and she was made a saint for doing something that most moms would do for their kids—I would hope. I know that's not true, but I would hope people would do that for their kids."

Emily drew encouragement from Saint Gianna's example throughout her pregnancy and the initial stages of motherhood. Emily's stay at the Home not only prepared her to bring a child into the world but helped her discern the type of work she wanted to do for a living.

"I've worked in child welfare for pretty much the last five years," said Emily. "My time at the Home definitely impacted me. I wanted to be an adoption social worker because of what they were doing at Saint Gianna's. I eventually decided on being a foster care case manager — that is what I do now. Saint Gianna's impacted that — my experience there turned into working with kids who are in unsafe situations. I know how close my kid was to being any one of these kids. I see the situations some of these kids come out of, and I know that easily could have been my child and me if I hadn't had a safe place to land. I think that's why it's critical to have maternity homes, and I wish there were more. If a place like Saint Gianna's can save even one mom and child from being homeless or having an awful outcome, I think it's worth it."

Emily's child Enya is nine years old. After nearly a decade, Emily looks back on the experience of an unplanned pregnancy and sees how much of a difference her brief stay at the Home made. While the Maternity Home does not promise outcomes for residents, it does promise support and respect. In Emily's words, it's a "Catholic-based safe place for women who are needing a place to land during their pregnancy."

"There's so much that I want to say, but there are no words that adequately sum up Mary Pat or Saint Gianna's or even come close," said Emily. "She's such an amazing woman, and it's an amazing place."

The Saint Gianna Way: Kate & Dominic's Story

Kate moved to the Home at the age of eighteen after unexpectedly becoming pregnant.

"I was not on very good terms with my family, but my mom found the Maternity Home through a friend," explained Kate. "I had nowhere to go and nowhere to be. I don't know how they convinced me to go, but I went. I was living with friends because I had gotten kicked out of my house. I was

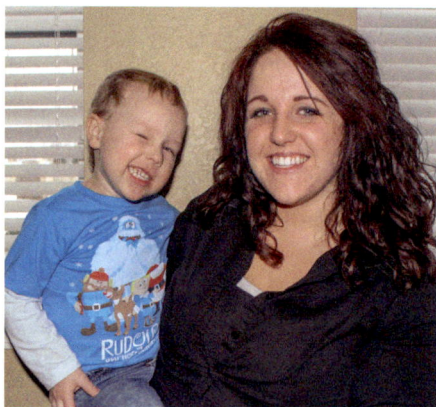

Kate holding her son, Dominic.

living out of a garbage bag. My friends were sweet to me, but you can't really raise a baby in that situation. Well, you can, but I wanted more. It was a God-thing. I just knew I wanted a better path for my kid than the one I was living."

Kate had been raised Catholic, but was not practicing the faith at the time she became pregnant. Despite being Catholic as a child, the move to Saint Gianna and Pietro's was a big adjustment.

"I was nervous and a little intimidated," said Kate. "It was rule-based and very Catholic. I was raised Catholic, so I was used to that part; but it was very secluded. It was out in the middle of nowhere with other pregnant women you didn't know."

Looking back, Kate can see how this time spent away from the lifestyle in Wyoming provided an opportunity to redirect the course of her life. While living at the Home for two and a half years, Kate was challenged to make sacrifices and encouraged to spend time regularly in prayer. This experience deepened her faith and helped her develop a strong foundation for her family life even after she left the Home.

"I don't think I would have been the mom I am today if it wasn't for the Home," Kate said. "I've made a lot of mistakes over the last 10 years, but I don't think my faith would have been as important if I hadn't gone to the Home and really practiced it. It would be a very different way of life for Dominic and me. Dom grabs his rosary and wants to pray. Our time there really instilled faith in God and trying to live a good, holy life."

Moving to the Home involves immediate sacrifices including moving away from family and friends and living with new people.

"You had to be prepared to change your whole way of life," said Kate. "It's not easy. It wasn't easy living in Warsaw with no amenities and no cell phones. When I was there, I pretty much just hung out with the people there. You don't get to do whatever you want but so many blessings came along with it. It's strict, but it's worth it."

In exchange for giving up certain lifestyle freedoms and choices, the women who move to the Home receive the experience of Catholic family living. The way of living involves moments of joy that can only be experienced in a home setting.

"I remember all the cooking we did in the kitchen," said Kate. "Whenever I hear a Bill Withers song I remember dancing around the kitchen with Dena, Shirley, and Crissy. There were so many times like that — good times. I formed bonds with housemothers and other residents that are pretty unbreakable."

With a laugh Kate continued that she "learned to do the dishes really well there." The possibility of a state inspection required a more rigorous degree of attention while doing the dishes.

"I didn't have a cell phone to be distracted by," added Kate. "It was just Dom and I, and the other residents at the Home. It was so peaceful. After living there for two years, it made me appreciate what I have. There was a simplicity to it."

For Kate, the simplicity of that time helped her to see that you can pursue holy living in the world today. Saint Gianna became a role model — both of what motherhood can look like in the modern world as well as embracing the daily activity of life in pursuit of holiness.

"She was such a modern-day saint," said Kate. "She gave birth to Gianna Emanuela after she was given choices – she could take care of herself or put her baby first. I think all of it is so beautiful. I wonder what my life would be like if I wasn't influenced by that mindset, if I didn't have her story. I wonder what I would be like if I wasn't taught the Saint Gianna way."

Over a decade later, Kate's time living at the Home still influences her family. She continues to identify with the idea of living out the 'Saint Gianna way,' having learned that it is in one's daily life that one is able to pursue holiness.

"Dominic has had a very good and blessed life," she said. "I really credit it to God working through the Home for me. It felt like everyone was saying a single mom can't be a good mom, but Mary Pat, and Dena were always supportive of my decision to raise Dominic. When you're so young like that, it makes a big difference."

During her time at the Home, Kate completed schooling for massage therapy. When she moved out of the Home, she began her massage therapy practice at a chiropractor's office in a nearby town. Saint Gianna's challenged her to provide a better way of life for herself and her child, but also allowed her to finish schooling and begin working to support her family.

At the time of the writing of this book, Kate's son Dominic just turned 13. Kate is married and just had her second child, a daughter named Roma. Both she and her family stay in touch with the connections she made while living at the Home.

"Not very many people know I lived at a maternity home," said Kate. "Whenever it comes up, it's always such a positive thing. It's not negative. I'm just so thankful for that home and what they offered me. It's not a shameful part of my life at all."

Miracles Happen: Jourdan & Nora's Story

For former resident Jourdan, Saint Gianna's Maternity Home helped her witness the miracle of her daughter Nora. The experience of God's providence is not a foreign experience to the life of the Home. There are countless stories of generosity, timing, and connection that can be explained in no other way than as directed by God's hand, but Jourdan and Nora's story shows us in a special way that God is actively working in people's lives. Jourdan, who attempted to abort her baby, sees her daughter Nora as a miracle. Nora reminds Jourdan of God's faithfulness during a dark time of her life.

"I was actively using drugs when I found out I was pregnant," said Jourdan. "I didn't want to bring a child into that. I had already had a daughter before and placed her for adoption; I didn't want to go through that again, so the first thing that came to mind was having an abortion. I made an appointment for the two-day abortion procedure and drove to the Cities for the first part of the procedure.

Jourdan pictured with her daughter, Nora, on her baptism day.

After that appointment, we were supposed to stay in the Cities, but we went home instead. The guy I was with bailed on me, so I didn't go back the next day. I had started the abortion process, and I knew that whatever they put in me could lead to a really bad infection if I didn't stop the process. I went to the hospital in town and asked if they could just stop the process because part of me didn't really want to do it but the other part of me didn't see another option. The doctor laughed and said my baby wouldn't make it through the night; and if it did, that it would be messed up."

"At this point, I had to ask, 'What are my options?' My mom had found out about the Maternity Home and wanted me to go there. If I was going to stay pregnant, I knew I couldn't keep getting high, so I ended up leaving and moving into the Maternity Home. It was the day after Thanksgiving that my mom and step-dad dropped me off."

The following May, Jourdan gave birth to a perfectly healthy baby girl, whom she named Nora.

Initially, the Home was a place for Jourdan to avoid drug use while she was pregnant. She had lived at a boarding school previously and wasn't worried about living with people she did not know. However, she was uncomfortable with the Catholic nature of the Home.

"I wasn't into the Catholic stuff and the way things were," said Jourdan. "I was used to living with other people in a similar setting, but when it revolved around the Catholic religion, I wondered what I had gotten myself into. Mary Pat and I had a lot of conversations — about going to Mass, the night prayers, and the rosary. I really pushed back against this part of life there until finally one day I walked into the chapel and sat down behind Mary Pat. She looked at me like 'What's going on?' I said, 'Don't worry about me. Just go back to what you're doing.' I ended up getting confirmed while I was there."

As Jourdan lived at the Home, she experienced God's love for her and realized how deeply she needed to accept this love and learn to love herself in order to break her drug addictions and embrace motherhood.

"The Maternity Home is not what I thought it was," said Jourdan. "Yes, it's a home and there are rules and you live with other women, but they help you get in touch with what you're missing in life. They help you get on the right track. They make sure that you are healthy and ready to move out with your baby. My biggest takeaway was really just being a mother. Before going there it wasn't what I wanted to do. I didn't want to go through it again, and I didn't want to place another baby for adoption; but they taught me how to love, more or less. And they taught me to love myself because it goes hand in hand. You can't love someone else until you love yourself…But the Home made a lasting difference in loving myself and figuring out how to be a mom. The Maternity Home will never not be in the back of my mind. They're always there because without them I wouldn't have Nora. It's a part of Nora's story."

Jourdan calls Nora her "little miracle," given to her to help her believe that anything is possible with God.

"I am beyond grateful for the Maternity Home," said Jourdan. "I love the Maternity Home. I love the people and the board members. It is a really good place. Without them I don't think I'd have Nora. God put Nora in my life for a reason, granted that I veered off the path, but I feel God's hand working in my life…I've had to work hard and be open to it and let my faith do the work. Without God though, Nora wouldn't be here."

Jourdan works as a Personal Care Assistant in a nursing home and her daughter Nora is eight years old. She would describe the Maternity Home as "a home for women who may not know what to do while pregnant, whether they go the adoption route or mothering or are a little lost. Whether Catholic or not, it is a good place to go; they are there for you when you need someone. It can be scary and confusing, but in the end, that place is there for those women who need that help."

Finding Safety With Nowhere Else To Go: Heather and Augustine's Story

For former resident Heather, Saint Gianna's Maternity Home became a home for her at a time in her life when she did not have one.

"I really had nowhere to go when I got pregnant," said Heather. "I was working at a second-hand store, Saint Joseph's Closet, and one of my co-workers said he could put me in touch with a priest. That priest put me in contact with the Maternity Home. On Valentine's Day I moved there — they came and picked me up."

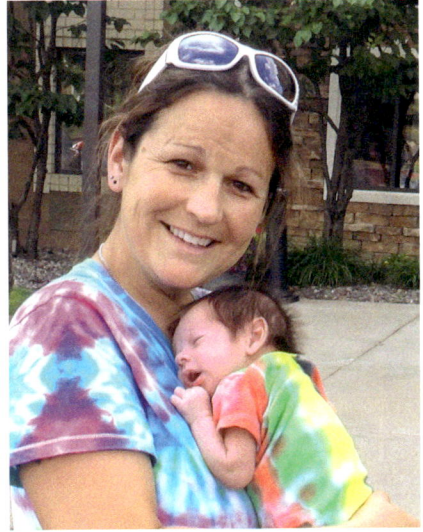

Heather holding her son, Augustine.

"I had some legal charges," said Heather. "I had gotten into trouble, and I was looking for help and answers. I was pregnant and really had nobody to turn to. They opened up their home to me."

Heather's experience at Saint Gianna's was marked by the feeling that she was home — she felt that the Maternity Home family offered her love, acceptance, and help when she was in need.

"That's where my son Augustine was born," said Heather. "We stayed there, and it was a nice, quiet place. There was good food and good people. I got baptized while living there. It was at the Easter Vigil, so it was pretty special.

"I learned a lot about the Catholic faith and the saints," said Heather. "The different saints and all the feast days were interesting. I was open-minded to what they had to offer and what they had to teach. Father Joseph and Mary Pat were good role models."

While at the Home, Heather also had the opportunity to focus on her education in a way she would not have been able to otherwise.

"I started school online through Dickinson State for equine science," said Heather. "I took online classes and kept up with my education. They helped take care of Gus while I was there, and they helped me with my schooling. I had a couple of tutors and the housemothers helped as well and proctored my exams."

Heather recognizes the gift it was to receive the sacraments, learn more about the Catholic faith, and further her education, all made possible by her time at the Home.

"It was nice to have that security," said Heather. "I had a safe place to be and I felt safe. If you're looking for support and you're alone and pregnant and have nowhere to go, you have to trust it's a safe place to go. Mary Pat and Father Joseph know what they're doing — they've been doing this for years."

Many years later, Heather still sees the effects of her time at the Home.

"It impacted my life," said Heather. "I still cherish the memories and the teachings. I learned a lot, and I am making better decisions for my children and me after having been there. I know faith is something I should instill in my children, just teaching them about God."

When asked about the biggest takeaway from her time at the Home, Heather was quick to reply.

"The unconditional love shown," said Heather. "I'm glad that the Maternity Home exists. You don't find that very often. They showed me that there are people who care out there, and they're saving babies. What is a better job than saving babies? I think that's very special and pretty cool, but it takes a lot of work."

Ripples in the Community

Looking back over the past twenty years, those who have worked or lived at the Maternity Home are deeply aware of the necessity of donors and benefactors who provide support—both financially and with their presence. Almost everyone interviewed for this book remarked on how little they felt they had given to the Home compared to what they had received in return. The words of the Gospel have proven true over and over, "Give, and it will be given to you; good measure, pressed down, shaken together, running over, will be put into your lap. For the measure you give will be the measure you get back" (Luke 8:38).

The Good Work of Saving Babies: Father Scott Karnik

Father Scott Karnik is a native of Veseleyville, ND, a neighboring town not too far from Warsaw. He remembers when Father Hils began to share about the work of Saint Gianna's.

"Father Damian Hils was pastor at Saint Stanislaus and my home church, Saint Luke's in Veseleyville," said Father Karnik. "He told me of his plans for Saint Gianna's because he wanted donations to get it started. I remember him saying to me, 'We are saving babies.' That always stuck with me. His remark affirmed my position that all life is sacred, not just the life that is wanted. No one should be sacrificed on the pagan altar of choice. So I have had a soft spot in my heart for Saint Gianna's for a long time."

Father Karnik would watch this work — the work of saving babies — unfold as Saint Gianna's Maternity Home opened its doors and began to serve women. For Father Karnik, the Maternity Home illustrated the pro-life mission and encouraged him.

"Saint Gianna's has affirmed for me the importance of good in this world," said Father Karnik. "It has affirmed for me that others are good and are faithful enough to roll up their sleeves and get to work doing good. All of the people involved with Saint Gianna's have been leaders to people like me, teaching me to be good, to search for good, to affirm good, and do good in this world. It has animated my Catholic faith. When I worked in the world, I would donate some money and also some produce from my garden. I wanted to help in any way I could, more so to express my support for being pro-life and to support the many good people who are personally involved at Saint Gianna's, who have made a sacrifice of their lives to help the unwed mothers who have no place to turn when they're pregnant or have given birth and have nowhere to go."

Eventually, Father Karnik would share an heirloom from his own family with the Maternity Home family. He had spent some time in the US Army Reserves stationed in Germany. While he was there he purchased a beautiful vase for his mother. After his parents' passing, Father Karnik gave the vase to the Maternity Home as a way to remember his family and the great love for children his parents had.

"It was my mother's favorite," said Father Karnik. "I wanted to give it to Saint Gianna's because I was going to the seminary. I had to give away a lot of stuff. One testimony about Mom and Dad is that they had (on earth and now in Heaven) a special love for babies and little children. They always noticed them in a loving way, if that makes sense. They were meant to be husband and wife to each other and parents to us three children. I wanted to give that vase to Saint Gianna's because of Mary Pat's and everyone's love for babies there. It is a testimony to my mother and father and their love for all babies. Babies and their mothers should feel loved and accepted at all times. Mom and Dad would do that, and the vase is a special, tangible testimony of their love for each other, for their three children, and for all babies and their mothers, married and unmarried."

This love was passed on to Father Karnik who recognizes that "all babies can offer is love."

"They offer and give the purest love that is possible," said Father Karnik. "The only form of love greater is Jesus Christ's Real Presence to us in the Eucharist. Babies and the Eucharist are two very powerful truths of God's love for us."

Father Karnik views his work as a priest as a way to do his "small part" in the pro-life culture. He categorizes the work of Saint Gianna's as the work in the trenches. It is this work that will change the tide by offering women the truth in love.

"Saint Gianna's Maternity Home is the antithesis of what our legal and political culture have foisted and forced upon us: that life is disposable and expendable if it doesn't meet the legal litmus test of 'Is it wanted?'" said Father Karnik. "Saint Gianna's is a testimonial that abortion and the culture of death must never be woven into the moral fabric of our country. It is a tangible sign and tangible testimony that all life is sacred and must be protected because God has a plan and a mission for every one of those lives. It is a plan of holiness and construction of God's kingdom here on earth."

Father Karnik's reflections speak of the necessity of the Home. His prayers for the end of abortion are always tied to his prayers for the continuance of Saint Gianna's Maternity Home and places like it. He recognizes that the end of abortion is only possible with the existence of places like the Maternity Home.

"Saint Gianna's Maternity Home is a light of Jesus Christ," said Father Karnik. "It always has been and always will be."

Anchoring Faith in a Tangible Mission: Board Members Grant and Jackie Shaft

The opening of Saint Gianna's coincided with the Shafts' return to the Catholic faith, unexpectedly anchoring Grant and Jackie's faith.

"Our involvement with the Maternity Home was in the midst of our spiritual awakening," said Jackie. "We were not committed to the practice of the faith. We just didn't know the Lord at that point, but He had blessed us with a good life and a good family. But sometimes He has to stir you up, and it's either through a joyful event or suffering. For us, it was suffering. My brother committed suicide, and it was a jarring event for all of us. Our youngest (of three children) was one. We had the kids in Catholic school at the time, thankfully, but it wasn't because we were Catholic."

"We just thought the Catholic school would be better," said Grant. "During this time Jackie was given a book about the Blessed Mother. It was a short read, and it was literally an overnight deal."

"It was exactly what I needed," said Jackie. "So it was through the Blessed Mother that I started my relationship with Christ again, and that was a great gift. I could really relate to Mary then. My suffering came through my Mom and Dad's suffering through the death of my brother. Through the Blessed Mother, I could relate to her because I saw the suffering she endured with her Son, Jesus Christ. So I read this book and my life completely changed."

Jackie's "overnight" conversion back to the faith would prove to be a great gift to their family, but initially, it would make their marriage and family life a source of difficulty and turmoil.

"I wasn't happy about it," said Grant, now, years later, with a smile on his face. "She just read this book over the weekend, and she was an entirely different human being."

"In one fell swoop I realized how far I had sunk and where I needed to be," said Jackie. "So it was really just a beautiful trajectory, but not an easy one. It was very, very difficult for Grant, and it was very troublesome for us in our marriage."

Grant and Jackie both dug in their heels and their next year was rough. Grant made appeals to have his "old Jackie" back while Jackie attempted to bring Grant along with her in the faith. During the next year (2002) the Maternity Home was hosting a fundraiser—the singer Dana was putting on a concert at the Chester Fritz. Jackie was invited to help with the planning and because of this involvement, Grant and Jackie were invited to go to dinner after the concert with several others involved with the Home, including Archbishop (then Bishop) Aquila and Father Hils.

"We went to the Dana concert and everyone went to the old Sanders restaurant after," said Grant. "Bishop Aquila was there and I came in — I kind of knew the priests a little bit because I was on the school board at Holy Family even though I wasn't Catholic. I knew a few things but still wasn't a part of the whole program, so I was walking in with the Bishop, and Bishop Aquila was asking me something. I said to him, 'I'm Episcopalian and my wife is trying to get me to become a Catholic, but it's more likely that you will become Episcopalian before I would become Catholic.'"

Rather than ignoring his wife's new company, Grant's certainty about the falseness of the Catholic Faith allowed him to engage freely with Father Hils, Bishop Aquila, and other Catholics.

"We were leaving that night, and I was thrilled," said Jackie. "He met Father Hils, and they're the same age, and they really connected. We got in the car and Grant said, 'Talk about being overwhelmed by the white collars, but I kind of like that one young priest [Father Hils].'"

A few months later the Shafts invited Father Hils over for dinner, and Grant accepted his invitation to come to Warsaw for his inquiry classes for those joining the Catholic Church at Easter.

"I think he knew I was pushing back on things," said Grant. "And he said to me, 'I don't understand this one thing — you have your kids go to a Catholic school. As a parent, as a dad, I'd think you'd want to know what these things are that your kids are experiencing.' And I said that makes sense. Catholicism wasn't super foreign to me because I was familiar with the Episcopalian High Church. He told me he had an inquiry class on Thursdays, and he said it just means learning. He didn't say it was the class you take to join the Catholic Church. So both Jackie and I went. Father Hils is an exceptionally gifted teacher. We went, and I loved it. In a matter of months, I went through the same thing Jackie did."

"My conversion was a lightning bolt to my heart," said Jackie. "My conversion was that I fell in love."

"Mine was the opposite," said Grant. "Mine was cerebral. I was convinced there was no way that this priest whom I kinda liked was going to get me. I would go to class, and I would spend the week in between reading through as many books as I could—all anti-Catholic apologetics. I just needed a couple of zingers for Father Hils when I went to class, but I was reading stuff and all of a sudden I started thinking, 'This protestant stuff doesn't sound right.' Slowly but surely over four or five months, I came to the conclusion that I thought Catholicism was right even if it sounds crazy."

Through their deep connection with Father Hils, the whole Shaft family grew in their Catholic faith and fell in love with Saint Gianna's Maternity Home and its mission. As they became involved, the mission of the Home was a guiding and illuminating light on their path to understanding what it meant to live out their faith.

"My brother died in 2001," said Jackie. "Grant came into the Church in 2003, and between 2002 and 2004, we became very involved with the Maternity Home. It's all so intertwined—the Home, the people there, and our return to the Church. The mission is so dear to our hearts. The whole mission of the Home became a part of our whole spiritual journey. We got to know these holy people and their witness to what they were doing was so important to us."

"It meant everything to us," said Grant.

God was working Himself into the Shaft family and a large part of this was through the presence of the Maternity Home and Father Hils. In the Home, Grant and Jackie found a pro-life mission that was not only true to the faith, but also very down-to-earth and tangible. The Home was filling the gap between the local needs and the Church. It was deeply attractive to Grant and Jackie as they sought ways to live out their newfound faith. Their involvement

Saint Gianna's Maternity Home's first baptism; Kassity Meade pictured with her godparents, Grant & Jackie Shaft, Father Hils, and Father Gardner.

with the Home became a family affair and offered healing as they sought to respond to God's call in their lives.

Grant and Jackie became board members together beginning in 2005. Later, Grant transitioned to the Board of Advisors and remains on the board to this day. Jackie remained a board member until 2021.

"I remember taking my daughters Francie and Madeline up to the Maternity Home," said Jackie. "We'd pull them out of school and go help. This was the beginning, and Mary Pat was still figuring things out. The housemothers were still new, and we'd go up and help with bathing the kids or playing with them. My girls loved that, and they still remember it."

Shortly after Grant and Jackie completed the inquiry classes and continued their involvement with the Maternity Home, Jackie's brother Jed and his wife Jennifer grew interested in the Catholic faith as well. They, too, met with Father Hils and found themselves on a path back into the Church that included the Maternity Home.

"We were really living in a grace-filled number of years there," said Grant. "Not only our conversion with our whole family, but then Jed and his whole family and then Jackie's mom, and a couple of sisters were more on fire with their faith. We had some neighbors who reignited their faith and got involved."

"It was because of the Maternity Home," added Jackie. "Even today we have Lutheran friends that have great love for the Maternity Home. They wait for their saint of the year, and they love the traditions. They are drawn to the goodness. Father Hils, Mary Pat, and now Father Joseph — they're all holy people. Holy people draw you in. You're drawn to the goodness."

Reflecting on this time, they recognize the graces that accompanied them. Their involvement with the Maternity Home's beautiful mission illuminated their faith and encouraged them as a family.

"It was really a special time," said Jackie. "It was such a springboard for us, and you don't realize it while it's happening. You get involved with different kinds of services, and you just don't realize how it's going to impact you. We have wonderful memories, and the girls [their daughters], in their own spiritual lives, have been so affected and impacted by the service the Maternity Home was providing."

Years later, Grant and Jackie recognize the fruit of their involvement with the Home in the lives of their children. They are quick to point out how their children have been much more committed to the pro-life movement than they were when they were younger, which they attribute to their exposure to the mission of the Maternity Home as they were growing up.

"It was living out the faith," said Jackie. "The mission—the sacredness of life—the whole pro-life mission of the Home was at the heart of it all, of course. I think that impact is carrying on in my girls and our son John. They're all just very involved — each of them. Each of them in their own way is committed to the pro-life cause."

"We've been spoiled because being on boards over the years has allowed the kids to be exposed to the Bishop more than you ever would," said Grant. "This and other types of things like when Saint Gianna's son, Pierluigi, and daughter Gianna Emanuela visited. These are things that you don't get to experience unless you're involved. It all helped this whole thing with our family move along. Even beyond the Home and its mission, we saw so many great things about the faith and it sprung from our involvement with the Home."

The Shafts have joyfully given their time and love to Saint Gianna's Maternity Home, yet when they reflect on the role of the Home in their life and in their faith journey, they feel indebted to the Home.

"We give so much less than what we get, spiritually," said Jackie.

"If we had to monetize it, we could never repay the Home for all it's given to us," said Grant.

"And continues to give to us," added Jackie. "In difficult times we rely on them and in joyful times, they celebrate with us."

Paying it Forward and Gifts that Keep Giving: Bernice Kram

Bernice Kram and her family met Mary Pat through the Fargo Catholic School network. While the faith was already important to Bernice and her family at the time, the mission of Saint Gianna's would take on a greater importance as their family grew.

"Mary Pat Jahner taught religion at Shanley High School," said Bernice. "Our daughter, Melissa, was fortunate to have her as a religion teacher. I was heartbroken to learn of her resignation because our son, who was five years younger, would not have that same wonderful experience that his sister had."

Bernice Kram, far right, and the Bell Bank gift presentation.

Bernice works at the Bell Bank of Fargo. She could not have planned for the ways that Mary Pat's presence in her life through her daughter's education and her career in banking would be intertwined, but God had His time of great grace. While she recognized it as a difficult time and an uphill battle, Bernice always encouraged her son and his girlfriend.

"Our son and his girlfriend had our full support during her pregnancy, but what about so many unwed mothers that have no one to turn to?" said Bernice. "It was hard on us, and this was something we never thought would happen to our family. Many of our family members and friends were very supportive, but with others, there was a sense of judgment. So, I know that Saint Gianna's could provide loving support to all who enter their doors, and their program is of great value."

It was during this experience that Bernice's workplace began a new program to encourage their employees to be active members of the community, working to make a difference.

"At my company Christmas party in December of 2007, an Oprah Winfrey look-alike arrived to announce that our company was starting a Pay It Forward Program (PIF), just like Oprah had previously done on her show," said Bernice. "The program stated that each full-time bank employee would receive $1,000, a video camera, and an extra day off of work to do something in the community. Prior approval and documentation of our story were needed when each employee determined a need in the community. I would lie awake many nights wondering and praying of how I could make a difference with my Pay It Forward gift that I was entrusted with by the bank."

After much consideration, Bernice felt she had received an answer to her prayers.

"It especially weighed heavy on me one particular night," said Bernice. "And after praying for our son and his girlfriend and our grandchild, it finally hit me! Saint Gianna's Maternity Home and Mary Pat could use the Pay It Forward help! I could not wait until the next day to go to work. A very good co-worker and friend of mine also had a very similar story. I told her all about Mary Pat and Saint Gianna's. If you know either one of us — we couldn't just hand over a check, we had to do something much different!"

By experiencing what it was like to support someone through an unplanned pregnancy, Bernice carried both the unborn and the mothers experiencing unplanned pregnancies in her heart in a new way. It spurred her to share with others about the need for Saint Gianna's and to band together with others to provide for these women through the Home.

"After much discussion, we decided to call Mary Pat," said Bernice. "We visited, and after finding out different needs, one, in particular, opened our eyes. They were in the process of building an apartment above the existing three-stall garage for Mary Pat. As a director of the Maternity Home, it was determined to be very important that she would be able to get away to her own environment but still be nearby. It is a very stressful but rewarding calling. We asked for the phone number of the contractor, and we called him. We introduced ourselves, told him about the wonderful Pay It Forward gift we had received, and asked about kitchen appliances, the furnace, plumbing fixtures, the toilet, a shower stall, garage doors, and more. All of a sudden the contractor said, 'Wait, who are you again, and what do you want to do?' He said, 'No one calls out of the blue and wants to do all of this!'"

"At this time we had $2,000 but with another employee joining our cause and a very generous business and others willing to give discounts, we grew our money to over $40,000! On the first visit to Warsaw, we had a trailer full. To name some of the items, we had a furnace, a toilet, a shower stall, fixtures, a refrigerator, a stove, a microwave, garage doors, gifts for future moms and their babies, diapers, and homemade quilts. We had Tupperware and baptismal gowns and more. I can still see the expression on the faces of the residents and directors of Saint Gianna's as the trailer never seemed to run empty! All were blessed in so many ways."

Through her experience with an unplanned pregnancy in her family, Bernice was moved to help others who did not have the support they needed, yet when she thinks back on that first year of receiving the Pay It Forward funds, she calls it "one of the best presents" she has ever received.

"The Maternity Home is close to my heart and has influenced me to assist not only with the Pay It Forward program, but also to spread the word of the good works of the Home," said Bernice. "My Pay It Forward story with Saint Gianna's was featured a number of times at the Bell Bank Christmas Party with a thousand people present. I have learned a lot by planning and by carrying out events to raise money for such a worthy cause. It is addicting — the more you do, the more you want to do! This is the Pay It Forward ripple effect."

Bernice's trust in God's ability and providence to multiply her humble efforts have invited countless others to participate in the life-giving mission of Saint Gianna's Maternity Home. Beginning with her own family's journey, it has become a bridge between the community and the Home.

"The Maternity Home has taught me the importance of the pro-life movement," said Bernice. "Life has always been very precious to me, but the need to spread the word in today's world is even more necessary than ever. Now with the nation's political landscape, it is most important that I keep voicing the pro-life message."

As Bernice reflects on the current culture, she recognizes the importance of being present to others and generous with the needs of those in our communities. It is faithfulness in these small ways that creates a "ripple effect."

"Saint Gianna's Maternity Home is located in the small village of Warsaw in rural North Dakota," said Bernice. "The Home is nestled in a quiet setting without a lot of outside distractions. It is close to schools and medical centers. It may have a small presence, but it has changed and saved so many precious lives. Their motto is: One mother, one baby, one family at a time. How fitting, just like the Pay It Forward Program, the Maternity Home also has a ripple effect."

This ripple effect benefits not only the women and children of Saint Gianna's but many others as well. Those who learn of the Home, support it, volunteer or go there to pray, find peace and encouragement in exchange for sharing their time, talent, or treasure. The ripple effect spreads to all those who are seeking God's will in their relationships and families.

"The Saint Gianna Shrine is within the walls of the Home," said Bernice. "Many come to pray for healing in relationships. Some visitors come as they enter engagement and married life. Some come with health struggles. Most who come here leave filled with grace, hope, and peace. Some also come to pray to conceive. There are many beautiful stories of life, adoptions, and informed decisions. Family values are instilled. There is such a peaceful feeling that overcomes you just by paying a visit — it's hard to describe!"

Bernice's relationship with Saint Gianna's Maternity Home has also spurred her on to continue voicing the pro-life message as well as paved the path to a connection she never imagined having.

"Never in my wildest dreams did I ever think that I would meet Gianna Emanuela," said Bernice. "And when I did meet her, all I wanted was a photo taken with her and to say a few words. That did happen, but later I was overwhelmed when Gianna Emanuela reached out to me and asked if I would accept an invitation to serve as a director of the Saint Gianna Beretta Molla and Pietro Molla Foundation. I have accepted this invitation to serve with great joy and gratitude! In my spare time, I have helped to raise funds, and now I am pleased to assist by being a director on the national board of the Saint Gianna Beretta Molla and Pietro Molla Foundation. God always has a plan, and we need to be patient, have faith and trust in him! Who knew that our grandson, the Pay It Forward Program, and Saint Gianna's would all be God's plan in this community? These are gifts that will never stop giving back. It's more than I could have ever imagined or felt worthy of!"

A Story and Saint That Could Really Happen: Sarah Effhauser

Mary Pat taught Sarah Effhauser theology while she was a student at Sacred Heart High School in East Grand Forks, MN. Mary Pat had taken a part-time job from 2001-2002 while working towards the opening of Saint Gianna's Maternity Home in Warsaw.

"Mary Pat only taught theology that one year, which is crazy to think about how it all lined up," said Sarah. "She was just at the beginning of the renovations."

During that same year, Sarah's mother Natalie Wavra received a series of life-changing news.

"She had a cancer diagnosis, and she also found out she was pregnant within weeks of each other," said Sarah.

Mary Pat shared Saint Gianna's story with the Wavra family as a source of consolation and intercession.

"It was very similar to Saint Gianna's story. Mary Pat was the first to say, 'Hey, do you know about this saint?' Saint Gianna really became a person our family looked up to, and my mom found solace in helping at the Home and being a part of the process," explained Sarah.

Various doctors advised Natalie to abort her baby in order to treat her cancer.

Finding herself in a similar situation as Saint Gianna, though Saint Gianna had a benign tumor and not cancer, Natalie took great comfort in the Saint's story, facing her pregnancy and cancer diagnosis with great trust.

"My mom was so young, only 34," said Sarah. "My mom and dad were a united front in giving the baby life. She did as much as she could while pregnant to treat her cancer. She had a couple of surgeries and did some forms of chemotherapy, and they delivered my brother, Gage, six weeks early so she could begin radiation. He was healthy and such a gift amidst it all."

"My mom went on to live nine years after that," said Sarah. "She passed away in 2011. From being told that she had just a few years to live, even with aggressive treatment, to seeing her live for nine years was truly a gift. Gage was such a driving force in her determination to live each day to the fullest. By giving him the gift of life, he really gave her back the gift to live hers as much as she could, for as long as she did."

Natalie's life was an outpouring of thanksgiving after having experienced the great sacredness of life and God's providence.

"My mom had such a giving spirit," said Sarah. "One year she asked if we could get the Christmas presents for the residents who were at the Home, so we started that and we've done that ever since. It was something she really looked forward to, and we still do it in her honor. She really felt that that was a way she could give back."

Sarah explained that the Saint Gianna and Pietro Molla Maternity Home concretely helps women in all areas of their life.

"I think it's so important because our generation — the generation to come is very pro-life, but Saint Gianna's is a way to bridge the gap," said Sarah. "Yes, we want abortion to be illegal, but we also want abortion to be unthinkable. And the Home stands in that gap between the two — as a tangible way that people can get involved in pro-life ministries. It also forms women; it's a place they can retreat to and find comfort and hopefully healing from some of the things that may have brought them into that experience. Life in all forms is important, and Saint Gianna's fills the need."

> "We want abortion to be illegal, but we also want abortion to be unthinkable. And the Home stands in that gap between the two – as a tangible way that people can *get involved* in pro-life ministries."

Oftentimes the language of "women's rights" creates a tension between the pro-life and pro-choice movements that should not exist. To be pro-life is to support women fully. Saint Gianna's Maternity Home models that in its mission.

"It tells them that you were created as a woman, and this is what that means," said Sarah. "There are so many people who have never been told what it means to be a woman and the amazing things we were created to do. That's one of my favorite things about Saint Gianna's — it's not just one baby — it's one baby, one mother, one family at a time."

Sarah views the life of Saint Gianna as a great example for mothers today.

"I was a working mom for many years, and I always had her to look up to for that," said Sarah. "I love the saints for those lofty goals of what they could accomplish. Saint Gianna was just so tangible — it's a story that could really happen. Thankfully I have the example of my own mother when hard things come up, you just make the next right choice and bind it in Church teaching."

The generous spirit of Sarah's mother inspired her in a deep way. Sarah and her husband, Matthew, have been blessed with six children. Their youngest, Rex, was adopted from Eastern Europe in the midst of the Covid-19 Pandemic. Sarah shared her own words on this experience in A Canticle of Praise Newsletter Spring 2022 issue:

Marriage and family life is often a delicate balance of 'yes' and 'no' as the couple and family discern where God is leading them as they journey towards Heaven. We write to you today as one of the many families that love and cherish the Saint Gianna Maternity Home. We have been married for fifteen years and we live with our now 6 children in rural East Grand Forks. We just completed an international adoption of the sweetest little boy with Down syndrome from Eastern Europe.

Sarah always had a heart for orphans throughout their marriage, especially those with Down syndrome, and although Matthew felt called to pray for them often, adding one of these precious children to their family was an entirely different calling. In the spring of 2019, we both knew it was time to make a step toward adoption and Sarah resigned from her teaching position to start the transition to being home full-time. The moments of discernment that ended in 'no' and 'not yet' were starting to turn into a 'yes' after years of patience and prayer. As each step towards adoption was met with consolation, we continued to look at profiles of waiting children. In late June 2020, as the world closed, we found the profile of the sweetest little boy waiting in Serbia and knew it was now our time for 'yes.'

Starting an international adoption in the midst of the pandemic is not for the faint of heart, and although we had our home study and dossier compiled in record time, and God opened so many generous hearts to help fund our adoption, it would still be an entire year before we would be invited to travel and bring our son home. A wait we never expected to endure.

On February 14th, we sat in a small playroom of his orphanage as we heard little footsteps and a gentle voice coming down the hall. As our sweet boy came around the corner into the room, his eyes were wide and curious. A whole new life awaited him and until this moment, he had no understanding of what was unfolding. Meeting, holding, and playing with our son for the very first time are moments we will forever cherish. The culmination of many, many prayers and the beginning of a new chapter in our family. We spent three weeks in the country to finalize our adoption and arrived home the first week of March.

As we spent our days in Serbia getting to know one another, we had an overwhelming sense of consolation that all the moments of 'no' along the journey, intertwined into our marriage and family life, were always for this 'yes.' Yes to making changes to our work-family balance. Yes to adoption amidst a pandemic. Yes to humbly ask others to come alongside us in prayer and financial support. Yes to opening our home to the lonely. Yes to waiting. Yes to our son.

Sarah holding her son, Rex.

We will forever be grateful to the Saint Gianna's community for their prayers and support. Not only is the Maternity Home a champion for the lives of mothers and babies that they serve, but they are also truly a champion for life.

As we settle into family life of 8 here in Minnesota, our schedules are bustling with sports, school, doctors, and therapy. Our days are full but our hearts are overflowing. There are plenty of hard moments but they are the hard and holy moments that build up the Domestic Church in family life. As our dear Saint Gianna said herself, "The secret of happiness is to live moment by moment and to thank God for all that He, in His goodness, sends to us day after day." And thankful we are.[10]

After Sarah's mother, Natalie, passed away in 2011, the Maternity Home's A Canticle of Praise Newsletter honored her life:

"Our task is to make the truth visible and lovable in ourselves, offering ourselves as an attractive and, if possible, heroic example." — Saint Gianna Beretta Molla

As Saint Gianna and other Saints have clearly shown us, holiness is lived in our ordinary day-to-day tasks, family life, and in all vocations. Our primary vocation is also a universal one; no one is excluded from the call to be a Saint and to be in Heaven one day with our Lord and all of His Saints. Blessed Teresa of Calcutta, when asked many times publicly to respond to the statement that she was a 'living saint,' would respond very simply that: 'To be a Saint is not the privilege of a few but instead the duty of each one of us.' We are all called to this holiness in our daily lives and to be an example that inspires others along this same path. Most of us have been blessed with a few people in our lives who stand out in virtue and encourage us to persevere and increase our hope and faith, especially when life is hard and God seems far away. Those of us at Saint Gianna's have been graced with many such people who have helped and supported us and continually renewed our dedication to the love of life and to support mothers who choose life. One of these people is Natalie Wavra.

This past July we received the sad news that Natalie had died. She entered eternal life on July 22, 2011. It has been almost ten years since I first heard of Natalie through her beautiful daughter Sarah. I had just moved to Warsaw and was beginning our work establishing Blessed Gianna's Maternity Home, while also holding a part-time job teaching religion at Sacred Heart Catholic High School in East Grand Forks. Sarah was one of my students. Toward the end of the school year, she told me that her mother had been diagnosed with cancer. At the same time, Natalie also discovered she was expecting a baby. I gave the family information about the life of Gianna Beretta Molla, believing that this great saint who is our patron, would certainly help them. Like Saint Gianna, Natalie Wavra loved life and she loved her husband and three children, but she also understood

that the precious little one growing inside her deserved life like the rest of her family. Like Saint Gianna, Natalie prayed hard and entrusted herself and her family to the loving arms of Divine Providence.

Natalie Wavra's family delivering Christmas gifts.

God blessed Natalie and her family with nine more years, years in which she welcomed her new child (Gage, now eight years old) as well as two granddaughters. They were years of difficulty and grace, a time in which she embraced her cross and suffering while finding joy in each new day. Many who knew her did not know the extent of her sickness or the toll it took on her because Natalie never focused on herself, but always generously gave of herself to others and to our Lord. Because Natalie recognized the gift of life, she was determined to use the rest of her life to grow in her relationship with God and to encourage others to do the same. One way that she did this was by forming a rosary group with other mothers, interceding for the needs of their families and of the Church.

Love and goodness naturally give of themselves to others, and it was no different in Natalie's case. Everyone who knew her was affected by the love and goodness that seemed to grow in her presence. Each year Natalie, along with her husband, her children, her sisters, and her mother, would 'adopt' the residents and even the former residents of our home. Close to Thanksgiving, I would receive a call asking for a brief description of each person's interests or likes. Then Natalie and her family, in the Spirit of Saint Nicholas, would shop and beautifully wrap and deliver the most heartfelt and touching Christmas gifts to Saint Gianna's, which we would then quickly hide until Christmas Eve when Saint Nicholas would leave these gifts for our ladies and their children. Year after year, after we placed the Christ Child in the manger of our Nativity Scene following Midnight Mass, we would all enjoy the love of Natalie and her family as each mother and child would unwrap gifts that were so special and personal.

Everyone here at Saint Gianna's has always felt loved at Christmas — and has felt the love of the Christ Child Himself — and this is due in large part to the spirit of love and giving that Natalie — whose name means Christmas — embraced in her life and shared with all she met. When the residents who have been here for a while help to welcome new residents, one of the things they always mention is Christmas, and how very special it is here at this home. Regardless of whom the Lord sends to us, we try to welcome our mothers and their children as if God is giving us an opportunity to welcome good Saint Joseph when he brought Mary to Bethlehem in search of a place for our Newborn Savior. Because Natalie and her family helped to make so many mothers and their children feel welcomed and loved, they have helped to make the love of God known to those who have not always been loved and welcomed. Natalie's husband, Michael, has asked to continue this tradition in Natalie's memory.[11]

Every Reason For Joy: Lynn Lane

Lynn arrived in Minto in 2006 after the grand opening of Saint Gianna's. She gives a unique insight into how the work of the Home has woven itself into the fabric of the community.

"My husband Nick and I have two children, Heidi and Jack," said Lynn. "We're not from the area which is a little unusual in this part of the state. When we moved here, I was oblivious to things going on since we weren't connected to the history of the town and the people here. But we heard about Saint Gianna's through Church and a few friends we made from Church."

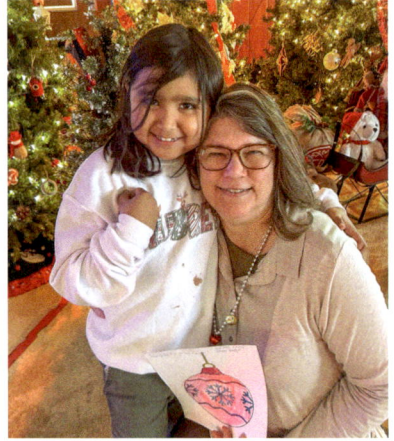

Lynn Lane with Aubrey.

Lynn's first contact with the Home came when she donated some baby items, but it would not be long before her friends would invite her into the life of the Home.

"Mary Pat was hosting a retreat day for her staff and residents," said Lynn. "She asked a friend of mine to babysit and my friend invited me to join as well, so it was three of us friends who babysat the kids that day at the Home. My friend Vicki gave Mary Pat my name then, saying Lynn loves babies if you need help with babysitting, so that's how that happened. We've had a few occasions where little ones would come over, some more than others depending on life situations, but then, when Aubrey was born, we were on a pretty regular schedule. That's when our bond really developed with the Home."

As a homemaker, Lynn found she had more time to share as her kids started school, and this coincided with getting to know Mary Pat and the Home.

"I really looked at this time on my hands as a gift from God," said Lynn. "I felt like He was leading me to volunteer in this way. It was like He was saying, 'You're available and there's this need, so this is where I want you to be.' And so it was a great gift to me."

As Lynn grew more involved, her whole family was able to connect as well.

"My children loved it, too," said Lynn. "My son is really good with little kids, just playing with them and adoring them. He has a strong connection with them. My daughter is a little older, and she's willing to be a part of it as well. It's been a good thing for our family to have little people around us. We're a small family, and this helps teach the kids about patience and having to wait. My husband and I came from big families, so that was familiar to us but not so much for them."

Beyond her family, Lynn also sees how the work of the Home makes a difference in the communities of Warsaw and Minto.

"I see them not only taking care of moms and babies but also taking care of the elderly in the community," said Lynn. "They're bringing meals to them, and they are being a witness to the value of life—really all life. They love people at all ages and stages, and I think it's important for people to see that."

Lynn's life of faith has been deepened by witnessing this ministry in action and opening the door of her home and allowing others into her family.

"Aubrey's adoption and sharing in her life has been monumental in our lives," said Lynn. "And Mary Pat has taught me a number of things. She has shown me how to celebrate other people. She is the 'hostess with the mostest'—she finds every reason to celebrate, every reason for there to be joy. I think that's good in the world we live in, especially now because it's easy to be downtrodden and depressed. She celebrates feast days and birthdays, and she knows how to celebrate. This has been a good message to me. She's been such a friend to us and has taught us a lot about love."

The Embodiment of Faith: Jed & Jennifer Carlson

Jed and Jennifer Carlson were introduced to the Maternity Home and Father Hils through Jed's sister Jackie Shaft. As they grew familiar with the Home, their family was forever changed.

"When you got involved with the Home, you felt like you were part of a family," recalled Jennifer. "As we came back to the Church, we started going to Warsaw for Mass with Father Hils. Our boys were altar servers for him, and we would have brunch at the Home after Sunday Mass. It was just part of what we did on Sundays."

Jed and Jennifer Carlson with their grandchildren.

For the Carlson family, the work of Saint Gianna's Maternity Home embodied the Catholic faith. In getting to know Mary Pat, Father Hils, and the staff, they found a support system of prayer for their family and an example of how to faithfully love.

Their involvement expanded from going to brunch on Sundays to Jed sharing his talents as a builder in an extraordinary way, by building the garage and apartment behind the Home. Jed and Jennifer even opened their home as foster parents and helped a mother with her young daughter.

For Jed and Jennifer, those at Saint Gianna's carried out the faith in a very ordinary way yet were able to touch countless people. This example served as reinforcement for their children as well, revealing that the faith they professed demanded a lived-out response.

"The mission of the Home is so important because it is the opposite of our culture," said Jennifer. "It gave our kids a deeper understanding of the faith."

Remarking that her children have more faith than she ever had as a young person, Jennifer views the work at the Home as having made a lasting impact on her family. Their daughter, Jessica Knutson, now serves on the board of the Home and the entire Carlson family remains involved to this day.

"It's not just the babies," said Jennifer. "It's the women, too. The Maternity Home is a place where women can feel loved; feel self-respect, and they feel safe. It is holy ground."

> "
>
> "The Maternity Home is a place where women can feel loved; feel self-respect, and they feel safe. It is *holy ground*."

The Power of Prayer: Brad and Wendy Simek Family

In giving us the Saints as role models, the Church teaches us that faithful prayer is essential in cultivating a deep and intimate relationship with God.

Brad and Wendy Simek attribute the growth of their family to the power of prayer, especially those offered at Saint Gianna's. Even before prayers were being offered for them, the Maternity Home held a special place in their hearts.

Brad's mother, Shalley Simek, served as State Regent for Catholic Daughters of North Dakota from 2000 to 2005. During this time, she fell in love with the Saint

Gianna and Pietro Molla Maternity Home's mission and began to advocate for its opening.

"She was responsible for helping raise funds for getting the Home started," shared Brad. "There's the stained glass window in the Chapel from the Catholic Daughters, and she was involved with all of this from the start. She was there when the Home opened, and it was a big deal for her. She really took it to heart, especially in her role as state regent. She really believed there needed to be a home in the state of North Dakota for mothers. So, I've known about the Home since before it existed."

Brad and Wendy Simek family with Father Joseph in the chapel.

Brad's mother passed away in 2005, shortly after the Home opened, which led Brad to keep Saint Gianna's close to his heart as a way to honor his mother. As parishioners at the Cathedral in Fargo, Brad and Wendy became friends with Father Joseph Christensen prior to his work at the Home.

"We always wanted to have a family, but we were unsuccessful," said Brad.

"There was no medical reason why we weren't successful," added Wendy. "There was nothing wrong."

During this time Father Joseph was the spiritual advisor for Saint Gianna's in addition to being stationed at the Cathedral in Fargo.

"We started going to the Home every once in a while when Father Joseph became the spiritual advisor," said Brad. "We'd talk with Mary Pat and connect. We were struggling with having children and the idea of what to do and looking into adoption."

"Father Joseph was praying for us, along with everyone at Saint Gianna's," said Wendy.

"Father Joseph left to go home for Christmas," said Brad. "This was the year we conceived, and we had just finalized our paperwork with Catholic Charities. We had gotten the phone call that they were going to start our home study the next January or February. We got a blizzard that year, and we were stuck, and Wendy said that she just didn't think something was right. Since we were having struggles, we made sure to get a doctor's appointment right away, and the doctor did an early ultrasound. They identified that Wendy was pregnant. They said to come back and make sure the baby's actively growing."

"So we went back, and the first time we went back, they told us that we were having twins," said Wendy. "And we had to go back every week until we heard the heartbeat."

"The second time we went back I was watching the ultrasound," said Brad. "I had become well versed enough to know what was what by this point. I asked the tech, 'Am I counting this right? Did you miss something last week?' And we went from having two to having three. We went from being elated, and then it was twins, and then straight to triplets."

"We were scared," added Wendy.

"The next week we heard the heartbeats," said Brad. "Father Joseph had come back from Michigan, and we met him in the sacristy. He said he had a vision about us — that he knew we were going to make good parents at some point. He told us not to lose hope. I said, 'That's funny, Father Joseph. We have something to tell you.' So we were telling him and Father Wilhelm that we were expecting and I said, 'But it's not just one — we are expecting three.' Father Joseph laughed and he shared another story with us."

Father Joseph explained how a couple of months prior he had kept praying with Mary Pat and the Home that the Simek family would have a child. Father Joseph finally thought about it and said, "God, why should you only give them one? Give them a family — give them children."

"My joke to him is, 'Couldn't you have clarified and said children over time, not all at once?'" Brad shared, as he and Wendy laughed.

Wendy gave birth to three healthy children — Gianna, Olivia, and Jackson — who spent only one month in the NICU before they were strong enough to go home. The life and work of Saint Gianna's remains an important part of the Simek family life. Their children know the stories of prayer that went into growing their family. Brad and Wendy have taken their children to the Home a number of times, both to share their story and to show their children the Home. While these visits have happened less frequently over the years, the role of the Home remains prominent in their family life.

All three children were confirmed by Bishop Folda this past year, with Olivia taking Saint Gianna as her confirmation saint.

"We're not full circle yet," said Brad. "But it seems like we're on that path."

A New Baby and Conversion: Ryan and Robin Wall

Ryan and Robin Wall were completely changed by their experience with Saint Gianna's Maternity Home. They were struggling to conceive and were almost certain they would not have children. It was not until Grant Shaft, someone Robin worked with, invited them to visit Saint Gianna's that they learned of this Saint, her story, and the work of the Home.

"I don't really know how Grant even came to know that we were struggling to conceive," shared Robin. "But somehow he did know, and he said he knew of this place and maybe we'd want to come there and pray sometime. Ryan and I agreed so we set up maybe three or four different times to go but none of them worked. Finally one day it worked out, and we met Grant and Jackie at the Maternity Home. They introduced us to Mary Pat and Father Joseph. We prayed, Father Joseph blessed us, and they gave us some prayers to say at home. We walked around, and they shared Saint Gianna's story with us and then we went over to visit Saint Stanislaus."

At the time, the Walls were unsure of what their future held. They did not know if they were going to pursue adoption.

"We were getting ready to leave and Devan [a resident at the time] was standing there," said Robin. "We just started chatting with her and didn't really think anything of it. She didn't look pregnant at all. We were getting ready to go and said goodbye to her. And I'll never forget it as long as I live, she looked back at us and waved. We were both sitting in the car, and I looked at Ryan and I said, 'We are going to adopt her baby.' She was very early in her pregnancy, and we didn't really know her but I just knew it."

"We had talked about adoption, but we weren't anywhere near starting the process," said Ryan. "It was something in the back of our minds, but when we left the Maternity Home that day, we just felt that it was going to happen. I felt the same way."

A few weeks later the yearlong celebration of Saint Gianna's ten-year anniversary was continuing with a banquet in Fargo. Mary Pat invited the Walls to come.

"We formed this bond with Devan immediately," said Robin. "A couple days later Mary Pat and Father Joseph said that Devan had expressed interest in adoption and that she was very interested in us being a part of that."

Sharing in the 2014 Christmas issue of A Canticle of Praise, Devan gives us her perspective on this experience:

"I found out I was pregnant in February of 2014 and thought my world was ending; now I can look back and see that God had plans for a new beginning for me. I moved into the Saint Gianna's Maternity Home that same month with a firm decision to choose life for my baby, but uncertain of anything else. A couple of weeks after moving into Saint Gianna's Home I met an amazing couple, Ryan and Robin, who had come with friends to visit Saint Gianna's to pray. We were introduced, and I think both of us thought immediately there was something special about the other. We developed an amazing relationship, and as I progressed in my adoption decision, they began the process to be able to adopt. They were a part of my pregnancy and many exciting moments, and I knew they were the perfect family for my daughter. My perfect little girl was born on October 17th, 2014; and from the moment I saw her, I loved her.

Newborn Rylee, who was placed for adoption with parents, Ryan & Robin, by her birthmother Devan.

Actually, I loved her from the moment I knew she existed inside me, but I was only sixteen, and that is why I chose adoption: not only for me but for her. I love her with my whole heart, but Ryan and Robin could give her a home as a married couple, happy parents who were ready for a baby, and the responsibilities of parenting her. They will always be a part of my life and in my heart and prayers."

At the time Ryan had written his thoughts to accompany Devan's in the newsletter and the following quote is taken from his reflection from that time:

"It was a cold day in the middle of the 2014 winter when Robin and I made a trek up to Warsaw, ND. The trip was planned to visit Saint Gianna's Maternity Home and pray to Saint Gianna for help with our infertility issues. This was our first of many trips to the Maternity Home, and it's burned into my memory. We visited with Father Joseph and Mary Pat, and Robin's friend, about our challenges over the past several years. We prayed to Saint Gianna in the Chapel and visited the rest of the Home. After a quick tour, we went across the street to take a peek in the chapel, and once we finished that short tour, we started walking back toward the Maternity Home. Mary Pat was walking towards us with this young girl, smiling and glowing. This was the first meeting we had with Devan. It was brief, five minutes, but afterward, both Robin and I knew that our meeting had a purpose. And that purpose was our beautiful little girl, Rylee Jayde. Prior to meeting Devan, we had only discussed adoption a few times in passing. Our intent on visiting the Maternity Home that day was to pray for our own struggle with infertility. After meeting Devan for those few brief minutes, we knew adoption was now our path. The Maternity Home provided an opportunity not only for us to become parents, but to give us another gift: the gift of an extension of our family. Our adoption is an open adoption. Because of that, we have grown to love Devan. Through her pregnancy we've spent many hours together, getting to know each other, sharing past memories, and talking about creating new ones. We've had the opportunity to meet her family and spend time together with them at their home as well as ours. Robin and I both think of Devan not only as the birth mother of Rylee but as a daughter."

While Ryan and Robin had always professed the Christian faith, their experience of adoption through Saint Gianna's moved them to a deeper belief.

"It's the best story," said Robin. "I tell people about our story all the time. Anybody that is questioning their faith or doesn't believe should talk to us. I grew up Catholic and Ryan has since converted. We were believers but it wasn't how it is for us now. I know without a shadow of a doubt that this happened because of God. There's no other explanation."

A few years later, the Lord surprised the Walls again when they found out they were expecting.

"It just happened," said Ryan. "We were pretty settled in at that point that we would just have Rylee and we were content."

After Ryan and Robin learned the story of Saint Gianna on that first visit to the Home, the saint has been a source of inspiration and encouragement for their family. Ryan, who converted to Catholicism after their adoption experience, chose Saint Gianna as his patron saint.

"When our son Reed was born we wanted him to have a connection to the Home as well, so we asked Mary Pat if Father Joseph could baptize Reed there," said Ryan. "We're all connected to the Home."

"There is something to be said for stay-at-home moms, but Saint Gianna has been such a huge inspiration for me in my working life as well," said Robin. "She didn't stay at home. Her career was really important to her, and mine is very important to me. I am a mortgage loan officer and work with a lot of first-time homebuyers, and I love it. I often look to her as an example of how to handle situations."

The Wall family's experience with Saint Gianna is one that has formed both their life at home and their relationships with others. Both Rylee and Reed have pictures of Saint Gianna in their rooms. These serve as a reminder to them and all who enter their home that Saint Gianna is a major part of their family life. Ryan and Robin are happy to share their story with others as well.

"I take the 'Warm the Winter' raffle tickets with me to work," said Ryan. "I walk around and tell people the story of Rylee and sell tickets. We always sell a ton. I think places like Saint Gianna's give mothers an opportunity to succeed when they wouldn't otherwise have one. It's a place they can go and get everything they need — resources, tools, support. It's awesome."

"With Devan, she sought out the Maternity Home," shared Robin. "There was a lot of pressure for her to not have her baby, but she sought out the Home. It's a testament to the Home and to Devan. Saint Gianna's gives young mothers another option. For someone who is scared but feels in their gut that they can't get rid of their baby, it is an option that gives them everything they need to succeed."

Having come to know Devan as an extension of their own family, Ryan and Robin view the work of the Home as necessary in today's culture.

"Even more than being a preventative of abortion, I admire the Maternity Home's work because they stick with the mothers after birth," said Robin. "And the ones who choose to parent their children, they teach them how to do it. I think many women who go there don't always know — they don't always have examples or family to help. That part of the work is so important — if they choose that path, they have the tools they need to succeed."

"In today's society people think about abortions, but they don't think about the other side of it," said Ryan. "There are pregnancy centers and places like the Maternity Home. There are options."

Ryan and Robin have felt the continuing support of Saint Gianna's over the years. From texting back and forth with Mary Pat to prayers to sharing about the Home, the Walls recognize the Home and Saint Gianna with a sense of permanence in their life — a bulwark of faith they never expected. Their life has become irreversibly intertwined with the Home and Saint Gianna.

"We didn't even know it existed, and it completely changed our lives," said Robin. "So if we can be the voice for someone else — provide life to another baby who otherwise might not be here, that's what we want to do by sharing our story. It's not always the most popular thing socially and everyone has different views or may be different from us, but we will advocate for it for the rest of our lives."

Being Open to Life at All Ages: Joe and Tiffany Johnson

The spiritual birthday of the Saint Gianna and Pietro Molla Maternity Home is December 12th, the feast of Our Lady of Guadalupe. On that day in the Jubilee Year 2000, Father Hils and Mary Pat Jahner had their first conversation about starting a maternity home in Warsaw.

Joe and Tiffany Johnson married in 2008, but it was years before they were blessed with children. In 2012, Joe and Tiffany had asked Joe's parents to pray for them to have children — either biologically or through adoption. Joe's parents took this prayer intention with them as they made a pilgrimage to the Our Lady of Guadalupe Shrine in Wisconsin.

"It was around 9 months later that we adopted Isaac," said Joe. "We found out about it, and it all was pretty fast. It was March when Leslie [Isaac's birth mother] called us, and then he was born in June of 2013."

While waiting for Isaac's birth, Leslie also invited Joe and Tiffany to be the godparents of her older son Gabriel. During her stay at Saint Gianna's Maternity Home, both Leslie and her son Gabriel were baptized. Joe and Tiffany formed a relationship with Leslie, opening their hearts and home to adopt Leslie's child while also welcoming Leslie into their family.

One year later in 2014, Gabriel joined his brother Isaac in Joe and Tiffany's home under their guardianship at the request of Leslie.

"What I've found with open adoption is that you are basically making the child and the child's family part of your family," said Joe. "You are getting to know them and they get to know you, and I think that's been really important for us and for the kids."

A few years later Joe and Tiffany made their own pilgrimage to the Our Lady of Guadalupe Shrine in Wisconsin. They wanted more children so they united their prayers to a spirit of openness to life, and once again asked for the intercession of Our Lady of Guadalupe. A short time after this they were asked to adopt Ruth, born to Tiffiny McKay, in 2017.

"Before we got Isaac my parents went on a pilgrimage to the shrine in Wisconsin," said Joe. "Then Tiffany and I went in October before Ruth was born. In each instance we didn't have an adoption plan even on the books, then we did these pilgrimages, and all of a sudden these babies came. Tiffiny had an adoption lined up with another family, but that didn't work out. I think she called in December and asked us if we would adopt Ruth and all of a sudden we were. We were asked in December and in January she was coming. It was really exciting, but it was like a gift out of nowhere. We weren't expecting it. Ruth was born January 13, 2017."

As the Johnsons adopted children, they realized that God was growing their family in a larger way. After the unexpected death of Tiffiny McKay in 2019, Joe and Tiffany welcomed Ruth's older sister Caliona into their home.

"We had kept in touch with Ruth's biological siblings through the years," said Joe. "It's been an incredible experience to have the two sisters together and the two brothers together. It's been really cool and so special — for them and for us."

The experience of adoption and getting to know the birth families of their children taught Joe and Tiffany a new way of being open to life in their marriage.

"I would just say be open to all possibilities," said Joe. "Be open to all possibilities and all ages. I didn't really have any experience with adoption coming into it, but for me, it's really been a growing and fulfilling experience. The more you get to know their families, for us at least, the more you realize how many kids need help — not just newborns."

Because of their relationship with Leslie and Tiffiny, the Johnsons view the work of Saint Gianna's as essential work both for the pro-life movement and for fostering families. When they reflect on the mothers who move into the Home and receive support, they view them as family members they must love and create a home for.

"The work is truly pro-life," said Joe. "You support these women during a time that can be difficult, and there's not as much support as you think. You think there are all these programs, but at the end of the day, there's not a home. It's a home, but it's also a place of formation and a way to succeed. It's structure. I know for both moms, they cried at the adoption ceremonies. It was a huge sacrifice for them. Both Tiffiny and Leslie, but it was with love, and I'm just eternally grateful to them for that sacrifice. It's probably the most selfless thing you can do, but at that moment they become part of your family."

By giving a home to women in need and welcoming them as family, Saint Gianna's offers the love and joy of Christ. These women become part of the Maternity Home family as well as members of other families they never would have met otherwise. It's a mission that has played a part in countless families, directly and indirectly.

Peace in the Adoption Process: Matt and Sarah Komprood

Saint Gianna's Maternity Home played an invaluable role in Matt and Sarah Komprood's experience of adoption.

"We were married in 2003 and we had Michael in 2007," said Matt. "We kept trying for more children which just wasn't happening. Once we came to terms with that we started looking into adoption. We did the home study with Catholic Charities and were on the waiting list for about one full year. In October of 2013, we were at a Catholic conference in Bismarck, and Mary Pat was there. She said she had someone downstairs that she wanted us to meet. So we went out of the talk we were going to and we went down, and it was Ella's birth mom, Jalen. That was the first time we met her. She had looked through our adoption profile book. She liked that we had a son because she had older brothers

Matt & Sarah Komprood family with birthmother, Jalen, and baby Emanuela.

and wanted her child to have an older brother. Then it happened really fast."

"It was really surreal, driving home with the adoption case worker following us and walking into our house with a brand-new baby," said Sarah. "It was a different way of becoming parents in so many ways."

This new way of becoming parents opened their eyes to the need for places like Saint Gianna's Maternity Home.

"It could have been very transactional but it's not; it was very relational," said Sarah. "I think it goes back to the heart of the relationship. I'm a nurse, and I see that so much in healthcare — we get people in the hospital, patch them up and send them on their way, but the ones who truly get better are the ones who truly have a community and team working with them. The Maternity Home is similar to that. They have a relationship that's so holistic instead of just offering monetary support or material items. It's making relationships with people and addressing the spiritual needs they have, especially with Father Joseph there. They are creating a community where people are accepted but also helped to improve in the ways that they need. I really appreciate that so much with Mary Pat, Father Joseph, the housemothers — all those involved — the way they help people, moms and dads, and the whole family — it's all on the table there."

Matt continued, "It's taking care of the whole person, and I could see that when we adopted Ella. We could see that Jalen [her birth mother] was taken care of. She was in a much better place than she had been before, and it's such a gift to not come from a place of crisis and emergency. The Maternity Home empowers women to do the best for themselves and their children. It's a whole different picture. It gave us a lot of peace as we went through the adoption process."

After Jalen's daughter, Emanuela, was placed with the Komproods, Saint Gianna's Maternity Home also served as a place for Jalen and her family to come together and spend time with Matt and Sarah's family. The Home's continued presence in the lives of the mothers and children who live there is a blessing and a true testament to the way the Home operates: starting with the love for Christ and extending outwards to share that love with families.

In the Christmas 2013 issue of A Canticle of Praise, the story behind Emanuela's name was shared:

Emanuela was born to Jalen, who chose a beautiful couple to adopt her infant daughter. The couple had been praying for quite some time through the intercession of Saint Gianna to be able to have another child. Jalen chose the name Emanuela Rose for her unborn baby, and the adoptive parents, Matt and Sarah, graciously accepted this beautiful name for their daughter. Gianna Emanuela is the name of Saint Gianna's youngest daughter. Saint Gianna's husband Pietro chose this name to honor his dear wife and also to acknowledge that even in her death and on the cross, and in the hardship and struggles that losing his wife and the mother of his children involved, God was with them and working out all of the details, and using even the loss of his beloved wife for good. I am sure he could not have imagined at that time that one day he would be sitting at the Canonization of his wife — indeed God was with them even in this terrible loss. And now we see how the Lord has most mightily used Saint Gianna's life and death, her example and her intercession, to touch the lives and hearts of so many people. We are able to see the intercession of Saint Gianna in our residents, in those who come here for prayers, and even in far-reaching ways, in the lives and families touched through adoption. Jalen, the birth mother of Emanuela, heroically chose life despite difficult circumstances in her own life at the time she found out she was pregnant, and then selflessly and courageously chose to place little Emanuela Rose in the loving arms of Matthew and Sarah.[12]

Generosity Rooted in God's Love: Deacon Howard and Hertha Hunkler

Deacon Howard and Hertha Hunkler provide a generosity that endures the test of time. Refusing to be limited by earthly terms of time and quantity, their Christian love has provided generous means for Saint Gianna's Maternity Home many years after their passing from this life.

The Hunkler's story begins when Deacon Howard was a young man. His older brother discovered the Catholic faith and subsequently converted his siblings and his mother. Around the same time, Deacon Howard's future wife, Hertha, was also taking Catholic instruction on her own and converted prior to their marriage.

Deacon Howard and Hertha Hunkler.

Taking their new found faith to heart, Deacon Howard and Hertha set out immediately to build a life worthy of the Gospel. They were married in 1941 and their lives were surrounded by the Depression and World War II eras. Deacon Howard and Hertha made their home on the homestead where Deacon Howard was born and raised. Their successful farming and ranching supported their family, which included ten living children and more in Heaven.

The Hunkler family sanctified their daily lives by acts of faith, hope, and charity. The entire Hunkler family experienced a deep connection to the life of the Church that overflowed from their lives of prayer and community. Two of their children include Sister Marie Hunkler of the Benedictine Sisters of the Sacred Heart Monastery and Father Jerome Hunkler, a retired priest of the Diocese of Fargo.

Eventually, Howard would become a Deacon, serving the Church in a special way, as his children grew older. With eyes of faith, the Hunklers were able to see their family as a vital part of Church life and vice versa—that the life of the Church was essential to their love as a family.

Because of this, they were open not only to a growing family life but also to the needs of the greater community. The Catholic Church served as a model for charity and their understanding of compassion extended to all, beginning with those in the womb.

Deacon Howard and Hertha began donating to Catholic Extension, an organization whose mission is to "ensure that all American Catholics can practice their faith within vibrant faith communities."

Setting up a trust through Catholic Extension, Deacon Howard and Hertha were able to continue offering financial support to causes they supported after their death, as a family legacy. One of the benefactors of that trust is Saint Gianna's Maternity Home.

Their daughter, Sister Marie Hunkler, shares about the character of her parents:

"I grew up with good, faith-filled parents — they were both converts to the Catholic faith and so their faith meant so much to them, and they passed that onto us. Our family life was very important. We ate three meals a day together, which is almost unheard of nowadays. Our parents loved life and my mother was involved in Right to Life. My whole family was involved in Right to Life, and my mother would write letters to the editor in support of life and that kind of thing. They always financially supported anything involved with the Right to Life, and Saint Gianna's is certainly about life. Our parents set up an endowment fund and various nonprofits get funding from that — Saint Gianna's is always one of them."

Over the years, the Hunkler endowment fund has provided for countless items including fencing, landscaping, extending driveways, the outdoor staircase, water softeners, septic repairs, flowers for the grounds, a new printer, a phone system and so much more. All of these purchases are normal household purchases. For Deacon Howard and Hertha, they understood what it takes to provide a home for mothers in need and were happy to provide for many of the "behind the scenes" items that are necessary for daily life.

"My parents made sacrifices all their lives," said Sister Marie. "It's because of those sacrifices that Saint Gianna's is one of the beneficiaries. It was their lifelong wish to assist the charities that they value and cherish. They were always quietly doing good all their lives in a private way that even we as a family did not know. They taught us that things are not as important as giving to those who are in need. That was always done in our home."

Over the years, the Maternity Home family has felt the intercession of the Hunklers from Heaven for their work. It's amazing to think that over twenty years have passed since the deaths of Deacon Howard in 2000 and Hertha in 1997, but the choices they made in love for Christ and His Church are still generously blessing others.

Loving Your Neighbors: Kaylin Gudjates

Kaylin Gudjates has always been a neighbor of the staff and residents of Saint Gianna's Maternity Home. The Maternity Home opened when Kaylin was three years old and she has a faint memory of walking through the Home with her parents prior to the opening. It has always been a part of her life as she grew up just a few miles down the road.

Kaylin and Aubrey

"For me, it was really normal," said Kaylin. "It wasn't until I was older that I realized how rare a place like the Maternity Home is, especially now that I'm in school for social work and am learning about different programs. Before my sophomore year of college, I just thought it was a normal thing that there was a place like that in Warsaw and that people knew those places existed."

Kaylin has siblings who are the same age as some of the children of former residents, and growing up it wasn't uncommon for Kaylin to help with babysitting or go over to the Home to jump on the trampoline. From her point of view, it was just another home and another family. She remembers having some of the residents in her high school classes in Minto and helping babysit for them as well.

"That was my initial involvement, but once I graduated from high school, I was looking for a job for the summer," said Kaylin. "My mom talked to a friend who was close with Mary Pat and the Home took me on full time that summer as a housemother."

Kaylin ended up coming back for four summers in a row to be a housemother at the Home. She also learned of a social work program from a fellow housemother and decided to switch to this major during her sophomore year because of her experience and connections at the Home.

"When I worked there, I had a unique situation because I lived so close," said Kaylin. "I didn't live at the Home like most housemothers do, but I have always felt like I was part of their family as well. The Home does a really, really good job at making women who live there feel like it's their family, too."

As Kaylin learns about social work, programs available, and helping people in a systematic way, she increasingly sees the beauty and uniqueness of the Maternity Home.

"They do such great work," said Kaylin. "They have really helped so many people. Whether you're there for two months, six months, or two years, everyone who goes there knows that they have someone to turn to down the road or right away, no matter what their situation is. They are making sure that the women are getting all of their needs met, not just the situation of them being pregnant. They are getting resources emotionally, financially, and physically. I think that's why it's so important — they are looking at the whole picture, not just one part of that person."

"They literally teach the residents how to be part of a family," said Kaylin. "They teach them how to have good relationships and life skills. It's so much more than just having

> "They literally teach the residents how to be part of a family," said Kaylin. "They teach them how to have good relationships and life skills. It's *so much more than just having a place to live* while you have a baby."

a place to live while you have a baby. As much as the Maternity Home is for all these women who come to have their children and get their feet on the ground, it's also made a huge impact on my life. It's how I found my career. As much as it's to help them, it's helped me to be a better person, and it's brought me so much joy in my life. They are great people, and how they conduct their home is so unique and refreshing."

Prayers Answered: Travis & Rachel Bushaw

Pregnancy can bring so many emotions to an expectant couple, and anticipating the arrival of a new life can be overwhelming at times. At 20 weeks gestation we entered the ultrasound room with the expectation of hearing news of normalcy and health for our unborn child. However, we left in an emotional whirlwind of shock and disbelief. Our physician had delivered the news that our baby had so many health concerns that he/she would probably not make it full term, and if the baby did, he/she might live only minutes or hours. According to the ultrasound, our baby had multiple brain cysts and numerous heart problems, including an extra vessel and unequally sized chambers of the heart.

Travis, Rachel, and Gianna Bushaw with Pierluigi Molla.

He told us that, in the worst case scenario, it could be Trisomy 18, a condition in which a baby's physical features appear abnormal and their inner organs are in disarray. He also said that this pregnancy was now in the hands of our God above.

We knew we couldn't rely on medicine to help us, so we quickly turned to our Lord and to our family and friends for prayers. My sister had connections to the Saint Gianna's Maternity Home in Warsaw, North Dakota, and called the director, Mary Pat Jahner, for prayers. Without hesitation Mary Pat passed on to us relics of Saint Gianna, and I wore one around my neck and another around my growing belly. We asked everyone we knew to pray to Saint Gianna for her intercession before the Lord.

We realized quickly that Saint Gianna was in great union with Jesus, as we were witnesses to the hand of God in everything that was to take place. Our next appointment was supposed to be weeks away, and it was quickly moved up to the following weekend. The advancement of medicine showed us, through a 3D ultrasound image, that our precious child no longer had any heart problems and only one cyst remained on the brain, a cyst which the doctor said would dissolve over time, and that we had nothing to worry about. After the appointment my husband and I felt we were in the midst of a miracle and we knew it was because of the prayers to Saint Gianna. For the next 20 weeks of pregnancy we had great faith in our new friend in heaven. On June 18th, 2009, we gave birth to a perfectly healthy and beautiful baby girl and named her the only name we thought was fitting, Gianna Marie.

The Sacred Ground of Sacrificial Love: Robbyne Sands

As a lifetime resident of the Warsaw area, board member Robbyne Sands thinks that Warsaw has been graced by the presence of Saint Gianna's Maternity Home. A young mother herself when the Home opened, Robbyne recalls her joy at having the ability to do something beyond donating financially to the pro-life cause.

"I believe I was pregnant with my third child around that time, and I was a busy mom," said Robbyne. "I remember being approached by Mary Pat after Mass one day. She asked if I wanted to help in the office, and I didn't feel qualified, but I said sure. I wanted to help in any capacity I could because I thought Warsaw was very blessed to have them here."

After working in the office for around two years, Robbyne stepped down from that position and shortly after joined the Home as a board member, a role she holds to this day.

"I think the place where I feel most valuable is when I'm asked to spend time with the mothers or their children," said Robbyne. "I feel like that is the core or heart of our work. Our mission is just to serve the women and children. I've done everything from helping moms try to figure out breastfeeding, to babysitting, to running women to appointments, to being a godmother. I always go home feeling so fulfilled — I was able to do something today not only for our community but also for our world honestly. Life starts in the family."

Through her involvement, Robbyne has been allowed to walk alongside other young mothers, sharing her experience in motherhood and family life. In this way, she has been able to show countless women and children the joy and sacrificial love that accompanies motherhood.

When Robbyne thinks about the work of the Home, she thinks of the women and children who become residents during a crisis pregnancy and also what the Home offers to communities. Having grown up in Warsaw and having family involved in the faith and life of the convent and Warsaw prior to the opening of the Home, Robbyne can see how much the Home has to offer in terms of encouragement, prayer, and faith for the community.

"I think about my family and my own sisters with their experiences of pregnancy," says Robbyne. "The Maternity Home is a place you can lean on. You're always going to get prayers and support. Women come to be comforted, and the Lord does comfort them through the service of the Home. I think it'll be an amazing day in Heaven when we're able to look down and see all the things — all the hearts that have been touched that we don't even know about."

The presence of the Maternity Home stands as a beacon of life and encouragement for all who know of it. It gives people the knowledge that they do not stand alone as they face difficulties or hardships in life because of Christ's love.

Another special opportunity Robbyne has received as a board member that has profoundly impacted her is her involvement in two adoption ceremonies.

"I can't even express or describe in words what it is to watch that birth mother place her baby with a family who is so excited," said Robbyne. "There's so much emotion in the chapel, and it's like your heart doesn't know which way to go. To be a part of that — that is the root of the Home. That's digging deep into what we do — the women and their sacrificial love blow me away. It's the most beautiful thing I've been a part of and the hardest."

Robbyne's words remind us that the Maternity Home truly is holy ground. It is the witness to the experience of suffering and joy, beauty, and hardship that many women and families face. The world wants to offer quick fixes and the removal of pain, but the Maternity Home's work is a testament to the life-changing power of Christ's sacrificial love. This love, modeled through Saint Gianna, stands as a solid ground for the women and children who live at the Home.

> "The Maternity Home *truly is holy ground.* It is the witness to the experience of suffering and joy, beauty, and hardship that many women and families face."

"I entrust my children to Saint Gianna every day along with my husband and myself," said Robbyne. "I have a huge devotion to Saint Gianna, and she was calling me to this work at the Home. I think it's astounding how the Lord provides for every single need – a babysitter, a driver for an appointment, the gala a few years back, and renovations. He provides everything so you know that there's just a beacon of light in the Home. They need it, and I think it's because we're so faithful, and He knows that and sees that. All the work being done is sacred work, God's work."

Life is Beautiful: The Bianco Family

While many of the stories in this book are from the early years of the Home's existence, there are just as many that have come from recent connections. The Bianco family's story is one that has only become intertwined with the Home in recent years. It is clear that Divine Providence has brought us together for a beautiful purpose.

Dr. Michelle Bianco and her husband, Robert, met while at the University of North Dakota in 1995. Robert was a graduate student in biochemistry at the time, and Michelle was in the medical school program. They were married in the year 2000 and continued in their work in biochemistry and hematopathology.

Father Joseph blesses Michelle Bianco with Saint Gianna's relics.

Michelle and Robert wanted to begin a family, but for unknown reasons, could not conceive. Their journey in adoption included an 11-month wait before their first daughter, Anna, arrived. Around five years later, Elise joined their family.

"We were blessed to adopt because their mothers chose life," said Michelle.

Michelle continued her work as a physician at this time, while Robert stayed home with their children, creating the family life that they both valued.

In April 2021, Michelle began noticing that something was not right with her health. "I went to three doctors before I got someone to believe me and send me to neurology," said Michelle.

In October 2021, a neurologist in Fargo referred her to Mayo Clinic in Rochester, Minnesota, for further testing and consultation. It was at Mayo that she was diagnosed with the early stages of Amyotrophic Lateral Sclerosis (ALS), also known as Lou Gehrig's disease. The disease, for which there is no known cure, results in the progressive loss of voluntary muscle control.

"My type of Lou Gehrig's is Bulbar. It affects my speech and swallowing before it affects my arms and legs," said Michelle. "In my case they think it is familial, meaning that I inherited it. If I had had a biological child, I would have a 50 percent chance of giving the mutation, or bad gene, to the child." After her diagnosis, "it all made sense as to why we couldn't have kids. I think we were blessed twice."

It was around this time that Michelle was prompted to look into Saint Gianna's Maternity Home. She had learned of it from her daughter Anna's friend, who had lived at the Maternity Home when she was little while her mother was pregnant with her second child.

"Something drew me to look up Saint Gianna's, in the August newsletter, they talked about the house that Saint Gianna's was building to accommodate future staff living and that they were going to take a loan out [to build it]. And something just struck me, I felt led by the Holy Spirit."

The house that was being built on the grounds would provide more room and privacy for current and future staff members as well as offer additional meeting and office space.

"We want to best prepare for the future of Saint Gianna's Maternity Home, and a significant part of sustaining our mission is providing adequate and appropriate living accommodations for our staff," the August newsletter stated.

"After I came back from Mayo in November, I, through Jan [Nelson of Heartland Trust in Fargo], wanted to meet them," Michelle said. "As I told them, when I first met them, I said I'm not a saint, but I felt a connection with Saint Gianna as she was a physician and Italian, of which I am both, and pro life, obviously."

Saint Gianna's great love for motherhood resonated with Michelle, who embraced the role of mother in her own life.

Michelle chose to make a donation that covered the expenses of building the Home. The Home was dedicated to Michelle and Robert's daughters with a plaque that reads: "Welcome to La Vita é Bella. This home is dedicated by Robert and Michelle Bianco to their cherished daughters, Anna and Elise. May all who enter here show gratitude to God for life and for this home, bestowed through a gift from the Bianco family and the time and talents of those who

made it a reality. Indeed, Life is Beautiful".
(The Italian phrase "La Vita é Bella" means
"life is beautiful").

Michelle's hope is that the Saint Gianna and
Pietro Molla Maternity Home continues to
grow, recognizing that "having the house is
what is important for the mission here to
continue. It's not the only thing, of course.
There are so many people involved and
volunteers — but having the building and
space they need is important.

Michelle and Robert's family life has unfolded
in ways they never could have imagined, and
while there is indeed much grief and suffering
in it, God is showing them just how beautiful
life is. The La Vita é Bella house is a testament

*La Vita é Bella grand opening
celebration.*

to their faith and stands in witness to God's goodness despite hardship.

Unexpected Joy (along with Faith and Hope): Mary Pat Jahner, Kassity Kayleigh (Hope), Geianna Emilee (Faith), Aubrey Rose (Joy)

It is hard to put into words all that fills my heart;
there is so much to say, so much gratitude, and so
much joy. God has been unraveling a plan I never
imagined and continues to do so in my life and in
the lives of each person who encounters the Saint
Gianna and Pietro Molla family.

When I graduated from high school and college, I
had some definite plans and ideas about what my
future would hold. Many of my thoughts of my
ideal path to happiness included many things that
have never become a reality. In a million years I never
would have imagined myself moving to a tiny village

*Aubrey Rose Joy at 3 years
old when she was adopted
by Mary Pat.*

(Warsaw, ND), single, and helping to start and run a maternity home. I never
would have imagined that on top of that, in these circumstances, I would be truly

happy and truly content—I would have thought this to be impossible! However, this is true: I have nothing I imagined or prayed or worked for, and yet, all that I could hope for. I will certainly say that I am beyond grateful that God did not answer all of my prayers, but that He instead led me down unexpected paths, meeting many friends, situations and circumstances, allowing both success and struggles, and many unexpected situations that have shaped who I am today. I am grateful that God has a plan and in His merciful love gives us much more than we could ever hope for or imagine.

Through this most beautiful work, I have been able to be a part of something bigger than myself; I have been able to serve struggling women and children, and have been, in many ways, a mother to many in this way. I have met amazing people and friends and learned so much about the human heart and about the goodness and generosity of so many people. I believe that Saint Gianna and Pietro Molla Maternity Home brings out the absolute best of those who are involved in any way—from the beautiful staff to the incredible board of directors, to our faithful benefactors, our spiritual supporters, clergy, and the mothers and little ones who have called this Home their home. I have embraced and walked with people in some of their most difficult times, and I have witnessed firsthand how the fear and trials of this life can still be accompanied with joy when people feel the love of God and of others. I have seen such loneliness and grief, and I have also seen many hidden miracles—I have seen firsthand the working of God inside of people's hearts. I have seen smiles and many tears, and I have seen those tears turn into joy and strength and grace.

> "
>
> "I believe that Saint Gianna and Pietro Molla Maternity Home brings out *the absolute best* of those who are involved in any way."

In all truth, upon first moving to Warsaw, I did not think I would always be here; it was a bit small (very small) and very overwhelming. However, it was a beautiful cause and I was most inspired through the heroic example of our patroness, Saint Gianna. I was young and idealistic and blinded in many ways to my real calling. I thought I'd help for a few years and then a religious community of sisters would come and take over, and then I'd figure out what I'd do for the rest of my life. Well, we did get that religious community, but it came in the form of men – the Franciscans of Mary Immaculate and especially, Father Joseph Christensen. We have had our prayers answered beautifully with these men giving our mothers a holy example of fatherhood and brotherly love. Their generosity and faithfulness to the work here has helped us preserve the rich Catholic identity that is so much a part of our apostolate. But their presence still leaves much for me and our housemothers to do here with the mothers and their precious little ones. The answer to our prayers helped me stay instead of leave. I have seen so much good, and at this point in my life I can honestly say I would hope to be here for as many more years as they will have me and as God will give me. This is indeed beautiful work!

This poem or prayer was found in the pocket of an unknown confederate soldier, and though it would not be an exact description of my life, it is very fitting:

I asked God for strength that I might achieve
I was made weak, that I might learn humility to obey.

I asked for health, that I might do great things
I was given infirmity, that I might do better things.

I asked for riches, that I might be happy
I was given poverty, that I might be wise.

I asked for power, that I might have the praise of men
I was given weakness, that I might feel the need of God.

I asked for all things that I might enjoy life
I was given life, that I might enjoy all things.

I got nothing I asked for — but everything I hoped for
Almost despite myself, my unspoken prayers were answered.

I am among all men, most richly blessed!

Each mother and each child who has entered our home has brought great joy and has touched my heart. They have taught me more about the Lord's goodness, and about myself. However, in these twenty years God has given me three very special girls who have changed my life – you might say completed my life in a profound and unexpected way. It has been written about already in this book – the fact that we prayed for that one baby who would make all of the effort, work, and time worth establishing Saint Gianna and Pietro Molla Maternity Home. That long awaited first baby was Geianna Emilee Faith; but when her young mother,

Shanna, came to us, she already had a precious one year old, Kassity Kayleigh Hope. She arrived in April of 2004 along with her mother Shanna who was due with another little girl at the end of October. Kassity had just passed her first birthday and was so tiny with hardly any hair. She was already walking, and people were always amazed because she looked like a six-month-old. Kassity was mechanical minded from the get-go and could put things together or fix things from the start. She was our first little one baptized, which brought so much joy to all of us. Despite having mixed dyslexia, she graduated high school with honors in 2022. She is now studying construction electricity and has become a beautiful young woman. She is motivated and disciplined and an example to me in organization and dedication. I value her insight and opinions.

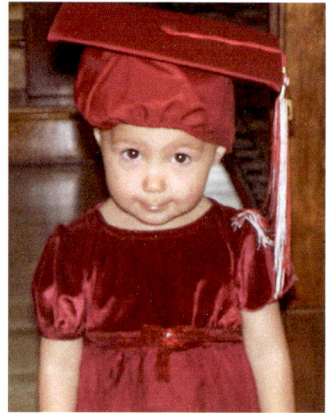

Kassity at her mother's high school graduation.

Kassity at her High School graduation, May 2022.

Then we have that first baby born here – the little one who made us all smile and cheer. Geianna Emilee Faith was born on the 22nd of October and brought so much joy to all who are a part of our Saint Gianna and Pietro family especially all who had worked so hard to see this day. To me she really was a gift from God, an assurance of God's blessing upon this endeavor in Warsaw. With her birth I could breathe easy — my heart burst with joy and pride with these two little ones in our home. Geianna has so much personality and a contagious smile; she is passionate and compassionate about life. She has given me an example of relating to people from all walks of life without fear and really being able to see the gifts in each person. She lives life to the fullest and is studying for a career in Radiologic Technology at Northland Community and Technical College.

Their mother, Shanna, was young. Even though she had a very difficult life, she really did grow during her time with us and felt the love of being welcomed by the prayers and efforts of so many people. She completed two years worth of high school in one and went on to a trade school after a year and a half with us. Because of her age, background, and the family we had formed, we kept in close touch and the girls were with us most weekends while that relationship and love grew. Life was not perfect for their mom as her past abuse and struggles gave way to addictions and mental health issues. She loved and still loves her girls; but the

Geianna at her high school graduation, May 2023.

capacity to care for her girls with her personal struggles became too difficult, and so we had Kassity and Geianna back with us to stay before they reached middle school. I cannot tell you how great of a gift this has been to see these beautiful "Maternity Home children" grow and develop and become the beautiful adults they are today. Growing up in a unique environment and being exposed to different people and difficult situations has strengthened them in faith and in

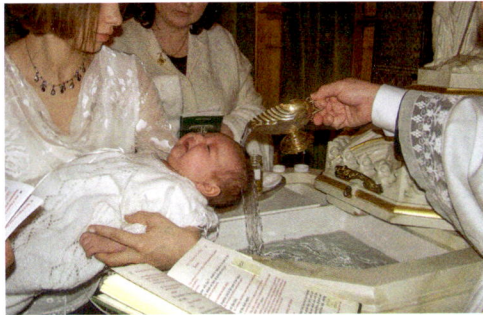

human skills. They are and have always been 'my girls', and I could not be more pleased. Although I never formally adopted them, and we all still maintain a good relationship with their mom – they are part of my family, a bond that God gave us, and they are my daughters in every way.

Geianna's baptism, December 12, 2004.

Another young mother who came to live at our home, and whose life would affect me more than I could realize, was Hannah. She came to Saint Gianna's in April of 2016. She was only sixteen years old, and six months pregnant. She had a great sense of humor, and we enjoyed the summer together with her little girl, Aubrey Rose, born on July 21st. When Aubrey was three months old, situations developed that required her mother to leave for another state, and little Aubrey was in the custody of the court. Hannah (Aubrey's birthmother) left on a Thursday, and we asked if Aubrey could stay, expecting that maybe she would be able to stay until Monday, and in that time, we could just give her a little more love and care. Well, as it turns out, Aubrey never left! She was just over two years old when I asked Hannah if she might consider letting me adopt her. She was still with us, and the longer the time Aubrey was with me, the more the bond of love grew. Even though adoption was not what I had originally thought or pursued, I felt strongly in prayer that it was right that she would join our little family with

her big sisters Geianna and Kassity here at Saint Gianna and Pietro's. I was already her godmother, as Hannah had her baptized when she was one, and asked me to take on that responsibility. At that time, I took her fully into my heart and promised to always pray for her. With time and also with what I had been through with Kassity and Geianna, I felt that God's will would be that we would be together here at Saint Gianna's. And through God's goodness, I was able to adopt her officially on October 30th, 2019. I added the name Joy to her name because she is such a great

Kassity, Geianna, and Aubrey.

source of joy to me and to all she meets. She is beautiful and loving; she loves to help; and she loves life, and animals, and the sun and outdoors. She is in second grade, and she is sensitive, generous, and loves to play. I cannot wait to see what God's plans are for her life. I feel so blessed to officially be her mother and feel complete in the gifts of Hope (Kassity Kayleigh), Faith (Geianna Emilee), and Joy (Aubrey Rose) that God in His immense generosity has given me. Indeed, I am blessed and most grateful!

The Magnificat

My soul proclaims the greatness of the Lord,
my spirit rejoices in God my Savior
for he has looked with favor on His lowly servant.
From this day all generations will call me blessed:
the Almighty has done great things for me,
and holy is His Name.
He has mercy on those who fear him
in every generation.
He has shown the strength of His arm,
he has scattered the proud in their conceit.
He has cast down the mighty from their thrones,
and has lifted up the lowly.
He has filled the hungry with good things,
and the rich he has sent away empty.
He has come to the help of His servant Israel
for he remembered His promise of mercy,
the promise he made to our fathers,
to Abraham and his children forever.

Luke 1: 46-55

Coming Full Circle

There are a few names and faces that have 'always been around' in the history of the Saint Gianna and Pietro Molla Maternity Home, including Kassity and Geianna Meade. These young women are the daughters of one of the first residents at the Home, Geianna being the first baby born while her mother was living at the Home.

In October 2004, the baby that would make "all of the work worth it" in the words of the late Bryan Grabanski, was finally born. Rebecca Crooks, daughter of Susan Barclay, remembers going to visit her in the hospital after being born. Her mother was

Rebecca with young Kassity and Geianna.

involved with the Home and, at the time, Rebecca was attending high school with Geianna's mother, who was the same age as her.

Who would have thought that, twenty years later, those children who first lived at the Home, ran through its halls, learned to walk, were fed, and prayed in its chapel would still be around, belonging to the Maternity Home family as they grew up.

"I don't really remember when I was here with my mom as a resident," said Geianna.

"Me neither," added Kassity. "I remember coming here when we lived somewhere else – we'd come on weekends or to visit. It always felt the same."

"I always feel safe here," said Geianna. "Everything is put together here to feel like family with everyone. I think one of the biggest values pushed here is trust. I think one of the good things about the Home is that if you struggle with something or are lacking, the Home will be helpful. Everyone would say something different. For me, it's trust, and the Home pushes me to trust. Mary Pat and the way the Home pushes me to be open to trusting other people and being open."

"I think one of the most important values at the Home is prayer," said Kassity. "There's a lot of togetherness. You do everything together – everyone goes to Sunday mass and night prayer. Everyone eats together and people don't usually do that anymore."

> "
>
> "There's a lot of *togetherness*. You do everything together."

Many of the mothers who come to the Maternity Home have previously been told they are not capable of having their baby or that it is not the right time. When mothers choose life for their babies, they are acting on the belief that their child's life is beautiful, despite the difficulty or hardship.

The work of the Saint Gianna and Pietro Molla Maternity Home bears witness to the slow, long work of goodness, evident in the children who have lived there. They grow into young men and women who have been given the most beautiful gift – life.

"I would say the Home gave my mom a reset button," said Geianna. "It was a place for her to slow down and think about what she's going to have to do with the rest of her life. Maybe she didn't plan very well, but she wouldn't have gotten where she is now if not for Mary Pat and the Maternity Home."

"Everything stays running because of the people," said Kassity. "Mary Pat said she has never taken out a loan because God will provide, and He always does. It's because of the people who have always donated or donated only once or donate every year."

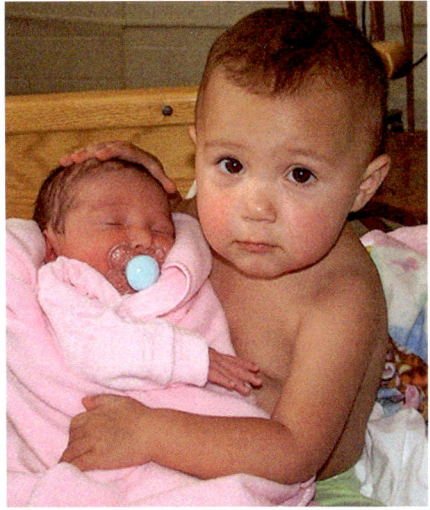

October 23, 2004: Geianna, our first baby born, 1 day old with her big sister Kassity.

"Growing up here and seeing the generosity of so many people, and experiencing their kindness to us, makes me want to be kind and generous and to follow that example. To the extended Maternity Home family, I just want to say thank you for being a part of the Home," said Geianna. "It really does make a difference here."

"Even if there is one baby saved, one baby saved from abortion, then it's all worth it!"

— *Bryan Grabanski.*

In Closing

It has been my privilege to document the history and stories that are in this book. What started as a daunting project spanning years and many phone calls has turned into the small memento you hold in your hands. It is meant to be a keepsake of these first years, but it also bears witness to the love of God in the world. In our world today it is easy to feel overwhelmed by darkness or confusion. But God's love is not abstract, moving in ways we cannot understand. It is practical and still unfolding in time. These stories are like little lights in the darkness – reminding us that prayer is powerful and that we can make a difference.

"The secret of happiness is to live moment by moment and to thank God for all that He, in His goodness, sends to us day after day." Saint Gianna

[1] Giuliana Pelucchi, *Saint Gianna Her Life of Joy and Heroic Sacrifice*, 38

[2] Pelucchi, *Saint Gianna Her Life of Joy and Heroic Sacrifice*, 45-52

[3] Pelucchi, *Saint Gianna Her Life of Joy and Heroic Sacrifice*, 89

[4] Pelucchi, *Saint Gianna Her Life of Joy and Heroic Sacrifice*, excerpt from letter to Pietro, 129

[5] Pope Saint John Paul II, *Tertio Millenio Adveniente*, §16

[6] Pope Saint John Paul II, *Tertio Millenio Adveniente*, §16

[7] *A Canticle of Praise*, Volume 1. No. 2 [formerly Gianna Home News] Nov. 2002

[8] *A Canticle of Praise*, Volume 2. No. 4 [formerly Gianna Home News] Dec. 2003

[9] *A Canticle of Praise*, Volume 13. No. 3 Fall 2014

[10] *A Canticle of Praise*, Volume 20. No. 1 Spring 2022

[11] *A Canticle of Praise*, Volume 10. No. 4 Fall 2011

[12] *A Canticle of Praise*, Volume 12. No. 5 Christmas 2013